LIFE AFTER GRADUATION

Financial Advice & Money Saving Tips

Terry Arndt, MBA
John Ricchini, MBA, CPA

Life After Graduation, LLC
5645 Kathryn Street • Alexandria, Virginia 22303
(877) 569-9816 (Toll-Free)
info@LifeAfterGraduation.com
www.LifeAfterGraduation.com

USING "LIFE AFTER GRADUATION"

"Life After Graduation" is the perfect product to be given as a gift, to raise money for a worthy cause, to increase an organization's membership, or to be used as a promotional device. In order to use "Life After Graduation" in one of the above methods, visit www.LifeAfterGraduation.com for more information or contact us toll-free at (877) 569-9816.

COPYRIGHT INFORMATION

BOOK DISCLAIMER

The authors of this book and Life After Graduation, LLC have made their best efforts in preparing this book to be accurate and complete. The content of the book is not guaranteed to produce any particular results. In addition, the advice given in the book may not suit every individual's circumstances.

Therefore, the authors and Life After Graduation, LLC do not assume responsibility for advice given. As a result, each reader should consider their own circumstances and abilities and weigh them versus the advice given.

The authors and Life After Graduation, LLC are not in the business of rendering financial, legal, or any other professional advice. If any questions regarding legal or financial advice should arise, the reader should seek professional assistance.

The authors and Life After Graduation, LLC shall not be held liable for any damages arising from the book's content.

DEDICATION

This book is dedicated first and foremost to our extremely understanding, patient and beautiful wives for all the late-nights and "chicken wing" get-togethers they went through, to Aspen for all the harassment he endured from Terry, and finally, to all the people who think we are the cheapest guys they know.

ABOUT THE AUTHORS

Terry Arndt and John Ricchini met while attending the University of Florida MBA program where they had both received a concentration in Entrepreneurship. While brainstorming for an idea for their entrepreneurial concentration business plan, Terry and John focused on the one thing they had in common, a strong desire to be frugal. The idea they developed was to create and sell a book containing financial advice and money saving tips for people who need it the most, the recent graduate.

Terry J. Arndt is currently employed as an Assistant Director of Membership and Marketing for a lobbying organization in Washington, D.C. Prior to his current employment, Terry worked as a sales representative for several years in the agriculture industry. During his career in sales, Terry attended a number of training courses in sales and negotiation techniques offered from world-renowned companies. Terry earned his MBA degree from the University of Florida and a Bachelor of Science degree from Washington State University.

John J. Ricchini is currently employed as a Manager of Financial Planning and Analysis at the University of South Florida Physicians Group. Prior to his current employment, John was a healthcare consultant at a "big five" accounting firm, a financial manager at a physician management corporation, as well as auditor with another "big five" accounting firm. John earned his MBA degree from the University of Florida and a Bachelor of Science degree in Accounting and Finance from LaSalle University. He is a Certified Public Accountant in the State of Pennsylvania and is currently pursuing a Charted Financial Consultant designation from The American College.

TABLE OF CONTENTS

TABLE OF CONTENTS

TABLE OF CONTENTS

TABLE OF CONTENTS

TABLE OF CONTENTS

TABLE OF CONTENTS

APARTMENTS

Trying to locate an apartment to rent can be an expensive and time-consuming task, especially if you are searching from another city or state. Even after finding an apartment, there are still a number of decisions to make. Therefore, whether you are searching for an apartment to rent, or you are already renting an apartment, you should review the suggestions and techniques listed below in order to save yourself time and money.

1. LOCATING AN APARTMENT ON THE INTERNET

There are a number of Internet web-sites to assist you in locating apartments in an effective and efficient manner. These web-sites allow you to search for an apartment based on numerous criteria, such as location, number of bedrooms and bathrooms, pet restrictions, and price range. To locate these web-sites, simply use any of the various Internet search engines available and enter the words "apartments" or "rent" in the search field.

These web-sites may offer toll-free telephone numbers in order for you to contact the apartment directly. If you do not have the time to contact each apartment directly by telephone, several web-sites allow you to request information on-line.

2. NEGOTIATING WITH LANDLORDS

The amount of negotiating power you have is directly correlated with the number of rental properties available. If there are a lot of properties available for rent, the better negotiating power you have. However, this does not mean that, if there are a limited number of rental properties available, you do not have any negotiating power. It simply means you must be more creative when negotiating.

Below are a few suggestions to assist in negotiating the rates of rental properties:

- If you are confident that you intend to live in a particular area for an extended period of time, consider signing an extended lease in order to lower your monthly rent or receive a significant discount on your first month's rent.
- When negotiating the terms of your lease, be sure to mention competitive rental properties in the area, specifically any promotional advertisements that a competitor is offering. Be sure to mention this even though you may prefer the apartment complex you are visiting. Let them know that you are an informed shopper and want to be given competitive terms.
- When negotiating the security deposit, if a full-month's rent or more is required as a security deposit, negotiate to have that amount reduced. If you are not able to receive a discount on your security deposit, request to have the amount of the security deposit paid in installments made over two or more months. Suggest this option even if you have sufficient funds available. This will enable you to have more flexibility with your funds when establishing your new home.
- When negotiating for a reduction in monthly rent or the security deposit, be sure to provide a reason for your request, such as the incredible financial strain you will incur by moving and establishing a new home during that initial month. Your reasoning may prompt the landlord to offer you the deal.
- Other negotiations can be made without discussing financial aspects. For example, you can condition your offer to rent the property on the replacement of new carpet or linoleum, or some other change. (Be sure to have any agreement put in writing).
- If you are signing a time-oriented lease (i.e. twelve-month lease), request to continue your lease on a month-by-month basis after the initial time frame of the lease has expired.

3. FREE-RENT PROMOTIONS

The competitive nature of the rental property market plays a significant role in the type of promotional offers a rental property offers. In a competitive environment, it is common to have rental properties offer the first month's rent for free or for a significant discount. These promotions generally occur in larger cities and college communities.

The free month's rent or reduced rent promotions may occur only during certain times of the year. Therefore, be aware of when these offers occur, as signing a lease at the right time may save you a significant amount of money. If you live a good distance from the rental property location, ask the landlord if they are currently offering such promotions. You can also contact the area colleges or the Chamber of Commerce to ask when, and if, such promotions are available in that community.

4. PREFERRED EMPLOYER DISCOUNTS

It is becoming more and more frequent for corporations, both large and small, to have a working relationship with rental properties. For example, an accounting firm that provides services for a property management firm may negotiate discounts for the accounting firm employees. Discounts can include:

- Waived application fee (usually $20 to $75)
- Reduction in the amount of your security deposit
- Reduction in, or waiver of, your first month's rent

5. REPAIRS/SERVICES FOR REDUCED RENT

Renting an apartment from a private individual has its advantages. Unlike most large apartment complexes that are owned by management companies and have an existing staff of maintenance employees, local landlords depend on local businesses to supply the repair services for their properties. This situation can result in a unique opportunity for the renter.

Due to the expense, time, and coordination of hiring local businesses to provide repair services, landlords are interested in alternatives to avoid this hassle. Therefore, if you have a fair amount of experience performing small repairs, such as painting or yard work, inform your landlord of your skills. You might be able to negotiate a discount in the rent during months in which you perform repair work. Do not sell yourself short for providing these services; however, do not become too greedy. Also do not agree to provide services you are not competent to perform, such as rewiring electrical outlets or repairing heating elements in a stove. You do not want to create the need for additional costly repairs.

6. SIGNING THE LEASE - A LEGAL PERSPECTIVE

The most important thing to remember before signing a lease is that, if there is a disagreement or conflict, all resolutions will be based on the legal document (contract) that you and the landlord signed. Therefore, if the lease does not reflect oral agreements that you made with the rental property management, it is your loss.

Below are some important steps to undertake prior to signing a lease.

- Read the lease thoroughly. In fact, it is recommended to take the lease and review it in private before signing it.
- When reviewing the lease, highlight areas on the lease that you are unsure about, or have questions regarding the meaning, and be sure to have them addressed.
- If the lease contradicts what was said to you during your meeting with the landlord, have them specify which version is correct – the lease or what was said. Be sure the lease reflects the correct version.
- If agreements are made regarding repairs to be made to the property or on what basis the security deposit will be refunded, be sure that the lease reflects those agreements prior to signing. For example, if the landlord states that new carpets will be put into the rental property prior to occupancy, be sure to write that term into the lease and have the landlord sign or initial that version before you sign.
- If you agree to a month-by-month lease once the initial terms of the lease are completed, have that specified in the lease.

7. MOVING INTO YOUR APARTMENT

You should follow these suggestions before moving into your new apartment:

- Always walk-through and review your apartment closely for all the items that are not operating properly or are defective prior to moving in. For instance, notify the landlord of stains in the carpet. Create a detailed list of all imperfections. Some rental properties have their own form for you to list damages on. If this form does not provide sufficient space for listing the damages, continue the list on a separate sheet of paper. Be as detailed as possible. Also be sure to note on the original form that a separate sheet containing further damages has been attached. Once you complete this task, sign the documents and obtain the signature of the landlord. Have two copies of the signed documents made - one for property management and one for you.

- If the apartment has not been cleaned or does not meet the specifications provided for in your lease, inform the landlord. Request that the needed services be completed immediately. Also request a discount or credit on your rent for the delay in your move and/or for the inconvenience you suffered.

8. MOVING OUT OF YOUR APARTMENT

The following are a few tips to follow when you are moving out of your apartment:

- Even if management does not require a "walk-through" of your apartment before you move out, request to have your rental property manager/owner walk through your apartment prior to your moving out, so that you are aware of any potential charges against your damage deposit.
- Once the walk-through is complete, request that the rental property manager/owner sign your damage report (that you filled out when you moved in) and state what, if any, charges will be deducted from your security deposit.
- Many apartment complexes will charge a standard non-refundable fee to have your apartment cleaned upon your departure. In almost all cases, this fee is stated in the lease and is usually reasonable and will guarantee that you will not be charged for any cleanliness problems.

9. SUBLEASING

Before agreeing to sublease your apartment, consider the risks you are subjecting yourself to. The laws in many states provide that the signer of the lease is liable for any damages that occur throughout the term of the lease while you are a resident, or after you turn the rental property over to another tenant under the sublease. Therefore, if the person to whom you sublease the rental property creates a significant amount of damage, (beyond what the damage deposit covers), and fails to pay for those damages, the landlord has the legal right to hold you liable for those damages. Therefore, instead of subleasing your rental property, consider finding someone that will sign a new lease. This will relieve you of all legal aspects of your lease. However, the landlord must agree to terminate your initial lease.

If the rental property manager/owner does not approve of starting a new lease with a new tenant in order to release you of your current lease, consider accepting the expense of terminating your lease early. Most leases specify penalties for terminating the lease. In many cases, terminating a lease early is far less expensive than paying for damages caused by a subleaser.

BANKING

Using a financial institution, such as a bank or credit union, to manage finances is something we all do. However, the use of banks and credit unions can cost a lot of money. Does it make sense to pay someone, in the form of various fees, to use your money? Of course not, but it is something many of us do. By finding the right financial institution to match your needs, you can save a significant amount of money.

1. BANKS & CREDIT UNIONS - THE DIFFERENCES

Banks
Banks are financial institutions that receive, lend, and safeguard money. Many banks also offer a variety of services, such as financial planning and safe-deposit box rentals. Banks can be divided into either local or national banks.

Local Banks
Local banks service a small community or region. They are generally owned and operated by members of the community in which they are located. Due to the nature of local banks, they generally offer services that specifically cater to the community where they are located. Local banks also tend to understand the needs of the customer. For instance, if a long-time customer of a local bank needed a short-term loan in order to purchase an airline ticket to see a sick relative, a local bank is likely to work with that person because of their relationship with the bank.

National Banks
National banks are financial institutions that are generally owned by investors. National banks offer many of the same services as local banks; however, because of their size, national banks can offer more services and

usually at a better rate. Due to their larger size, national banks have difficulty catering their services to local communities and often lack the ability to take personal circumstances into consideration when determining eligibility for financial services. Therefore, national banks will frequently develop a one-size-fits-all product, such as a "College Student Savings/Checking Program."

Credit Unions

Similar to banks, credit unions are financial institutions that receive, lend, and safeguard money. Credit unions also offer their customers a variety of financial services. The primary difference between a bank and credit union is that a credit union is managed and operated by a non-profit cooperative group. For example, state and government employees often have credit unions that they can participate in. Since credit unions are non-profit, they can offer very competitive interest rates on accounts and loans, and they frequently do not charge for many of the same services that banks charge for, such as using a non-associated ATM (Automated Teller Machines).

Because federal law regulates credit union membership, you need be part of a particular group to be eligible for membership. To determine if you are eligible to join a credit union, consider the following:

1. Contact local credit unions and ask them their requirements for membership.
2. Contact your employer to determine if they are associated with a credit union.
3. Ask your family members if they belong to a credit union. Many credit unions offer membership to immediate family members.
4. Some credit unions base membership eligibility on geographic location. Therefore, ask your neighbors about local credit unions you may be eligible for.

2. DETERMINING YOUR NEEDS

Understanding your financial institution needs is very important for two reasons. First, it is important to know what services to look for when opening an account with a financial institution. Second, it makes you aware of what fees you are currently paying and how to avoid paying those fees in the future.

To understand your financial institution needs, collect your bank statements for the past six months and complete the chart provided below.

Month	1	2	3	4	5	6	Average
Number of Checks Written							
Number of ATM Withdrawals							
Fees:							
ATM Usage							
Account Maintenance							
Overdraft							
Others: (describe each)							
1)							
2)							
3)							
Interest Rate on Savings Acct.							
Interest Rate on Checking Acct.							

Once you have completed this chart, evaluate your usage pattern. Visit with your current financial institution, as well as others in your area, to determine if there are methods that you can implement in order to reduce various fees or charges you frequently incur.

3. DIRECT DEPOSIT
Many financial institutions will waive monthly service fees for your account if your paycheck is directly deposited from your employer to the financial institution. Contact your human-resource or payroll office to determine if your employer offers this service.

4. INTERNET USE
Many financial institutions are offering account access through the Internet. To encourage customers to use this service and avoid using tellers, financial institutions provide incentives such as waiving normal fees for transfers or account inquiries. This service is very convenient and efficient for customers who can not travel to the financial institution's location for ordinary banking needs and that do not have the time to stand in line.

5. PRINTED CHECKS

Inquire about free printed checks from your financial institution as many institutions offer this service when you open a new account. If you need to purchase your printed checks, avoid purchasing them from your financial institution because the average charge is between $12 and $17 for a box of 250 checks. Instead, order printed checks from either a company on the Internet or from advertisers in the Sunday newspaper, as these tend to be less expensive then what a financial institution would charge. Furthermore, consider changing companies with each order you make. By doing so, you will receive "first-time ordering" discounts.

6. AUTOMATED TELLER MACHINES (ATMs)

When using an ATM, be aware of your financial institution's ATM usage fee, as some financial institutions will not charge a fee for using ATMs that they own. Other institutions, (commonly credit unions) will allow you to use ATMs at locations other than their own without incurring a fee. However, these financial institutions usually limit the usage of these types of programs. For example, the first 10 ATM uses per month are free, then each additional use is at a fee of $1 per transaction.

7. DEBIT & CHECK CARDS

There are several advantages and disadvantages associated with using debit cards. One advantage is that debit cards are easy to qualify for. As long as you do not have a bad credit history, you will most likely qualify for a debit card. Other advantages are that debit cards are more readily accepted than checks, identification is not required when using a debit card, and there is no need to carry cash or a checkbook.

One disadvantage of a debit card as compared to a checkbook or credit card is that funds are automatically taken out of your account. When using a checkbook or credit card, you are provided a slight delay in the transfer of funds or in the payment of the expense. Other disadvantages of a debit card are that it is difficult to record transactions, debit cards are likely to have fees associated with their use, and debit card statements do not normally offer a detailed list of purchases as credit card statements do.

BUDGETING

Saving money when you purchase a good or service, as discussed throughout many of the sections in this book, is quite different from saving money. One of the most effective ways to save money is by developing a personal budget and implementing it. Budgeting involves understanding where your money comes from and where your money is spent, saved, or invested.

Most people understand the concept of budgeting; however, very few people truly understand the benefits of budgeting. Budgeting is often viewed as a difficult, time-consuming, and boring task. Although budgeting can take some time, the benefits gained from budgeting are tremendous. From purchasing new clothes to planning your contributions for your retirement, budgeting will play a significant role in meeting all of your financial needs.

1. IDENTIFY YOUR FINANCIAL GOALS

Start a list of your top ten to fifteen financial goals. Create a list of short term (less than 1 year) and long term (2 or more years) financial goals. Goals can be anything that is important to you, such as getting out of debt, buying a new outfit each month, paying off all your bills each month, buying a new car, saving money for a trip, or even saving $50 a month. By establishing your financial goals, you create an incentive to stay focused on developing and maintaining your personal budget. Two charts for listing your short- and long-term goals have been provided on page 12.

2. RANK YOUR GOALS

Once you have established your short- and long-term financial goals, rank them according to their importance to you. This will be used as your progress chart. Make a copy of your goals and place them somewhere where you will see them frequently as a reminder.

Short-Term Goals

Goal	Expense	Time-Frame	Rank
Ex: New Clothes	$100	Monthly	

Long-Term Goals

Goal	Expense	Time-Frame	Rank
Ex: New Car	$3,000 down-payment	June 1, 2006	

3. DETERMINE YOUR INCOME

Determining your income is one of the easiest tasks of your budget. Income can be generated from a variety of resources, such as your salary, annual bonus, income tax return, commission, interest payments, or dividends. A chart has been provided below to calculate your income. **Use income you receive after taxes.**

Income

Source	Amount	Occurrence
Ex: Salary	$1,356	2 Weeks
Ex: Bonus	$2,500	Dec. 15
Ex: Interest	$20	Quarterly
Total:		
Average/Month:		

4. DETERMINE YOUR FIXED EXPENSES

Every month, as well as yearly, there are a number of fixed expenses you need to pay. Having an understanding of when these expenses occur will assist you in developing a budget that plans for these expenses.

When filling out the Monthly Fixed Expense chart below and the Yearly Fixed Expense chart on page 14, place all your known expenses where they occur and estimate where the others tend to occur. For example, on the Monthly Fixed Expense chart, place the cable bill on the 13th of the month. On the Yearly Fixed Expense chart, only list those expenses that do not occur each month, such as holiday gifts, automobile license fees, and magazine subscriptions. You will notice that the Yearly Expense Chart has a monthly average section, which means to take the total expenses and divide by twelve. This amount will be deducted from your income along with your monthly fixed expenses. However, this amount will be placed in a safe account, such as a savings account. As these various fixed expenses occur throughout the year, you will have sufficient funding available to pay for them.

Monthly Fixed Expenses
Examples include Rent/Mortgage, Cable, Auto Insurance, and
Loan Payments (automobile & educational loans)

1 Ex. Rent $500	12	23
2	13	24
3	14	25
4	15	26
5	16	27
6	17	28
7	18	29
8	19	30
9	20	31
10	21	
11	22	Monthly Total:

Yearly Fixed Expenses
Examples include Gifts (Holiday/Birthday), Automobile Registration,
and Subscriptions

January	Ex. Automobile Registration - $125
February	
March	
April	
May	
June	
July	
August	
September	
October	
November	
December	
Total	
Monthly Average (Total/12)	

5. DETERMINE YOUR VARIABLE EXPENSES

Determining your variable expenses can be difficult. Variable expenses include everything that is not included in "Fixed Expenses" and vary in their occurrence or expense each month. For example, groceries, snacks, entertainment, gasoline, long-distance telephone charges, and clothing purchases would all be included in this section.

To keep track of your variable expenses try some of these suggestions:
• Keep a small notepad/piece of paper and pen with you at all times to record where you spend your money.
• Request receipts for all of your purchases. Purchase duplicate checks or write a detailed description of your purchases in your check register.
• Spend a few minutes every evening to record your daily variable expenses.

- Spend an hour each week to review your daily variable expenses and calculate totals.

When filling out these charts you will notice a section for credit cards. All purchases made on credit are to be listed under the particular section where the purchase belongs. For example, if you purchase $10 of gasoline for your car on credit card, you would list $10 in the automobile section. The credit card section is to be used for those people who have prior credit card balances and may not recall what the expenses were used for. Place payments made toward that previous balance in this section of the chart. A separate section is located just below the credit card section to place any fees (interest, late, etc.) you may have incurred.

Provided below is a daily variable expense chart (for one week) and on page 16 is a weekly variable expense chart (for four weeks). Make copies of these charts as needed.

Daily Variable Expenses

	Daily
Automobile	
Household	
Snacks	
Entertainment	
Laundry	
Groceries	
Personal Care (Haircut, etc.)	
Medical (Dr. visit, etc)	
Utilities	
Credit Card	
Fees (Interest, Late Fees, etc.)	
Other:	
Totals	

Weekly Variable Expenses

Week	1	2	3	4	Totals
Automobile					
Household					
Snacks					
Entertainment					
Laundry					
Groceries					
Personal Care					
Medical					
Utilities					
Credit Card					
Fees					
Other:					
Totals					

6. PUT IT ALL TOGETHER

Once you have completed all the charts (a total of one month of budgeting), place the information you have gathered into the chart provided below.

Totals

Total Monthly Income (TMI)	
Monthly Fixed Expenses	
Yearly Fixed Expenses (Monthly Payment)	
Monthly Variable Expenses	
Total Monthly Expenses (TME)	
TMI - TME	

7. EVALUATING THE RESULTS

The results of filling out the chart above will provide one of two results regarding your financial status; you are either living within your means or you are not. The results also tell you if you are capable of meeting the financial goals you have established for yourself earlier in this section.

You Are Living Above Your Means

If the total from the "Totals" chart on page 16 was a negative number, you are living above your means. Beware, this is a very serious situation and should be addressed as soon as possible. The first thing to do if you are living above your means is to evaluate your budget. If there are areas in your budget where you can reduce your expenses, do so. In most cases, reducing your expenses is far easier than increasing your income. If you review your budget and there are no areas of the budget that can be reduced, then you may need to seek professional assistance.

You Are Living Within Your Means

If the total from the "Totals" chart on page 16 was a positive number, you are living within your means. This is a great accomplishment and you should be very proud of yourself. Not everyone is capable of accomplishing this goal. However, just because you are living within your means does not necessarily mean you are meeting your financial goals. To determine if you are meeting your financial goals, complete the chart on page 18.

Example:
Assume there is $500 remaining after all expenses have been paid. Earlier in this section, a short-term goal of $100 per month to purchase clothes was given. Another goal was to acquire $3,000 for a down payment on a new car to be used in June 2006. This example budget is starting January 2002. Therefore, this person has 53 months of about $55 each month to acquire the $3,000 needed for the down payment.

Remaining Funds (After Fixed/Variable Expenses)	Ex: $500
Goals:	
Ex: Clothes	Ex: -$100
Ex: Car Down Payment	Ex: -$55
Total Remaining (After Goals)	Ex: $345

In the example, this person is living within their means and is meeting their goals. On top of that, they also have remaining funds. Under this situation, this person should consider investing the remaining amount. For more information on investing your money, read the "Investing" section on page 67.

8. HOW OFTEN SHOULD YOU BUDGET?
When establishing a budget, you should complete all the sections/charts above for at least three consecutive months. Once you have completed those three months, you have done all the hard work. However, this does not mean you are done. Budgeting should become a normal part of your life. As you accept more and more responsibility in your life, the more important budgeting your finances will become. For example, when you purchase a home, start a family, or decide to retire, being capable of understanding your financial situation will be imperative. Therefore, at least once a year, as well as any time there is a major change in your lifestyle or financial goals (for example when you accept a new job or receive a raise in your salary), you should update your budget.

9. ADDITIONAL BUDGET RESOURCES
There are numerous resources available to assist you in developing and maintaining a budget, including books, software, and professionals. Regardless if you are having difficulty establishing a budget or you are an avid budgeter, you should seek out these additional resources. The more information you have about budgeting and the better you understand your financial goals, the more efficient you will be in accomplishing your financial goals. These resources can be found in your local library, a bookstore, the Internet, and many financial institutions.

CAR CARE & REPAIR

Everyone knows that car repairs are often very expensive. However, most people are not aware of the methods available to save themselves a significant and considerable amount of time and money when having their car serviced. This section includes valuable information on how to save a lot of money on preventative car maintenance and repairs and how to avoid feeling intimidated by auto mechanics.

1. THINK AHEAD

Listed below are suggestions to utilize in order to prepare yourself for the unfortunate, but unavoidable, occurrence of automobile trouble.

Join An Automobile Club

For a minimal fee, automobile clubs provide their customers with a variety of services, including towing and changing flat tires. However, before joining such a club, be sure to contact your current automobile insurance company to determine if you are already paying for similar services.

Purchase Windshield Protection

Consider purchasing windshield insurance if you live in an area where window chips occur frequently, such as in an area with gravel roads. Windshields are expensive to repair and replace yet these large expenses can be avoided by investing in windshield insurance coverage.

Take A Basic Car-Repair Class

Search your community for local colleges and organizations that offer basic car-repair courses for a small fee. You will learn the basics of car repair, such as changing a tire, starting a car with a dead battery, and changing your oil. You can also request the dealer who sold you the automobile to provide this information to you.

Assemble Or Purchase An Emergency Kit
An emergency kit includes basic tools, flares, jumper cables, a gas can, as well as other helpful items for when your car breaks down. These kits are a small investment that only takes up a small amount of space in your car's trunk. Emergency kits can be purchased from various locations, such as a car dealer or auto parts store. You can also save some money by assembling your own kit.

2. PREVENTATIVE MAINTENANCE
Preventative maintenance will stop problems before they start or before they worsen into situations that may be costly to repair. Listed below are some basic tips to save money on necessary preventative maintenance.

Change Your Oil
Changing your oil on a regular basis is probably the single most important preventative maintenance task. The necessity of oil changes may vary according to the make and model of your automobile, as well as the driving conditions in which the automobile is used. However, the general rule of thumb is every three months or 3,000 miles, whichever comes first.

Rotate And Balance Your Tires
Rotating and balancing your tires will extend the life of the tires considerably. Generally, tires should be rotated every other time you change your oil or every six months, whichever comes first.

To obtain these services for free, consider purchasing your tires from a dealer that provides a lifetime service program. These programs generally include free flat-tire repair and tire rotation and balancing for as long as you own them.

Alignments
Alignments are an easy way to extend the life of your tires. The recommended frequency for an alignment varies depending on your tires and the driving conditions. However, every four to six months is a good rule of thumb. Most locations that perform alignments will provide a limited warranty for free or for a minimal charge on this service, such as re-alignments as necessary within six months or 6,000 miles. These places also occasionally offer seasonal discounts on this service. These discounts

can reduce the expense of an alignment by up to one-third of the normal expense.

To get the most for your money, be sure to purchase an alignment with a warranty. Then remind yourself when the warranty on your alignment expires, such as noting the date on your calendar. Effectively, you will be getting two alignments for the price of one.

Tune-Ups
Your automobile should come with a book that suggests the timing for various preventative maintenance tasks. For example, your car manual may suggest a full "tune-up" every 50,000 miles. These tune-ups usually include changing spark plugs, changing/adjusting belts, adjusting the timing, filling various fluids, and checking your engine for any potential problems. If you do not have a manual, you can purchase one from a car dealer or an auto-parts store.

3. AUTOMOBILE REPAIR REFERENCES
A good method to save yourself a lot of money on car repairs and be satisfied with the service you paid for is to find a reputable service/repair shop. The easiest way to find these locations is to get references from a variety of people. The more people you ask the better.

If you are in a location where you do not have the luxury of asking acquaintances for references, (for example while travelling), then ask at auto parts stores, gas stations, or the local police station. If you are unable to obtain any satisfactory references, a national chain is usually a safe bet. In addition, ask if the mechanic who will be working on you vehicle has any outside certifications. Certified training from your vehicle's manufacturer is a good indication of a competent mechanic.

4. DIAGNOSING AN AUTOMOBILE PROBLEM
Recognizing that your car has a problem at an early stage is the first step to saving yourself a lot of money. Ignoring the warning signs could end up costing you a large sum of money in the future. Listed below are suggestions on how to properly diagnose your car's problem.

Get A Consultation
Once you start to hear noises or feel a difference in how your automobile drives, take your car in for a consultation. Many automobile service centers provide this service at no charge. However, some service-centers assess a fee, so be aware of the service centers terms before agreeing to a consultation. If your car is under warranty, take it to the dealership that honors the warranty.

Get A Second Opinion
Once the first service center determines what they believe the problem to be, ask them to describe it to you in detail, and in terms that you can understand. State that you will be getting a second opinion and you would like them to provide you with a written estimate for the repairs. Be sure to collect any information about warranties or specials that they are offering; then take your car to another location and follow the same procedure. If the second opinion is different from the first opinion, seriously consider obtaining an opinion from a third service center.

Do not feel pressured to have your car repaired by a service center just because they provided you a free consultation. Remember that the consultation was free.

5. CHOOSING A REPAIR SHOP
Once you have gathered all of the quotes as detailed above, review the results and choose the service provider based on the factors that are most important to you. Consider the following before making your choice.

Purchase The Repair Parts
Many auto repairs entail replacing a broken part. Ask the service center to tell you what parts are needed so that you can purchase them yourself in order to save money on the expense of the repairs.

Consider The Reputation
Be sure to consider the reputation of the mechanic/service center before choosing the lowest-priced location.

Consider Warranties

Take into consideration whether the service center provides a warranty for their work, especially if the car repair is expensive. Also be aware that warranties usually only cover the part being replaced, not the labor. However, some service providers will offer a discount on the labor if the auto part fails.

Consider Repair Time

Before deciding on a service center location, consider the amount of time it will take to have your car repaired. If the cheapest service center location cannot fix your car for two weeks, it may be worth the additional $50 to have your car repaired the next day at a different location.

CAR INSURANCE

The following are easy to follow tips that could save you hundreds of dollars each year off your car insurance premium.

1. UNDERSTANDING THE BASICS

Review your current policy and teach yourself about what each category of car insurance covers. Make sure you understand the following categories: liability, collision and comprehensive coverage, medical, personal injury protection, no-fault, uninsured/underinsured motorist, and other supplemental features (i.e. rental car, towing, and windshield replacement).

After reviewing your policy, if you still have difficulty understanding it, contact your current insurance company or another company and ask them to explain each category to you. Also, be aware that every state has minimum insurance coverage laws for automobiles. Be sure to have your insurance company explain what this means as well.

2. COMPARISON SHOP

The premiums from one insurance company to the next can vary greatly; therefore comparison-shopping is to your advantage. Although this can take some time and effort, it can ultimately save you hundreds of dollars. Therefore, this task should be completed at least once a year. To assist with this process, a comparison chart has been provided for you to use on page 27. In addition, there are a number of Internet web-sites and insurance companies that you can contact that will provide you comparison quotes.

3. REPUTABLE COMPANY

Make sure that the insurance company is a reputable firm that offers excellent customer service and will be able to pay any potential claims you may have. To avoid this, be sure to inquire of your friends, family and co-workers to determine their experiences with, and suggestions for, insurance companies.

4. DISCOUNTS

Inquire about the following discounts:

- Anti-theft devices
- Age discounts
- Marriage discounts
- Airbags and automatic seatbelts discounts
- Multi-car discounts
- Multi-line discounts (for purchasing several insurance policies)
- Safe driver discounts
- Good student discounts
- Defensive driver training course discounts
- Anti-lock brake (ABS) discounts
- Low mileage discounts
- Garage parking discounts
- Loyalty discounts (maintaining automobile insurance with the same company for a number of years)
- Car-pool discounts

5. HIGHER DEDUCTIBLE

A higher deductible should lower your premiums significantly. However, be sure to understand the consequences of a higher deductible. For example, if you were in an accident and had $500 of damages to your car, if your deductible is $500, then you will have to pay to have the repairs made. Deductibles usually range from $250 to $1,000.

6. PAYMENT TERMS

Discuss your payment options with the insurance company. Up-front payments or automatic deductions from your checking account may reduce your premium.

7. LOCKING IN GOOD RATES

If you are able to negotiate a good rate, attempt to lock that rate in for one year rather than a six-month period. Most insurance companies will review your driving record annually, and therefore by locking in your rate, you will prevent frequent premium increases due to traffic tickets.

8. TOWING PREMIUMS

If you already maintain a membership in an automobile club that covers towing, do not pay for towing coverage on your automobile insurance policy as well. If you do not have this coverage through an independent automobile club, consider adding it to your automobile insurance. This additional coverage is usually offered for a minimal fee.

9. WINDSHIELD COVERAGE

If you live in an area where windshield damage frequently occurs, ask your insurance company if such damage is covered under your basic insurance. If not, consider adding this coverage as it can be added for a minimal fee and can save you from making costly windshield repairs yourself.

10. NEW CAR PURCHASES

Prior to purchasing a new vehicle, inquire about the expense of the insurance. For instance, a sport utility vehicle (SUV) is more expensive to insure than an economy car. Also, the color and manufacturer of the automobile will adjust the expense for insurance. For example, a particular model of car may have a higher insurance premium if it is colored red versus white.

11. OLDER VEHICLES

Consider not adding collision and comprehensive coverage on vehicles that have a low fair-market value. The potential claim or deductible may not support the annual policy premium cost. Be sure to discuss this with your insurance company and have them explain the risks of not carrying this type of coverage.

12. CAR INSURANCE COMPARISON CHART

	Quote #1	Quote #1	Quote #2	Quote #2	Quote #3	Quote #3
Company Name						
Phone Number						
Contact Name						
Date of Quote						
Six-month Premium						
Annual Premium						
Coverage	**Premium**	**Limits**	**Premium**	**Limits**	**Premium**	**Limits**
Bodily Injury Liability						
Personal Injury Liability						
PIP (1)						
UM / UIM (2)						
Medical Payments						
Comprehensive						
Collision						
Rental Reimbursement						
Towing Coverage						
Windshield Protection						

(1) Personal Injury Protection
(2) Uninsured Motorist / Underinsured Motorist

COMPLAINT LETTERS & TELEPHONE CALLS

Complaint letters and telephone calls can result in both compensation and a feeling of satisfaction when the product you purchased or the service you received was inadequate. Situations in which you might write a complaint letter or initiate a telephone call are as follows:

- Poor quality food products from a grocery store or restaurant.
- Unsatisfactory service, such as from an auto mechanic.
- Products that do not meet your expectations, such as a new camera that will not work properly.
- Excessive charges for services, such as being overcharged for clothing alterations.

1. WHEN IS A COMPLAINT APPROPRIATE?

The easiest way to decide whether a complaint letter or telephone call is appropriate is to answer the following questions:

- Were my expectations met? This does not mean, "did the product/service work?" It means, "did the product/service work as I expected it to perform or did it perform better than I expected?" If the answer to this question is "no", then proceed to the next question.
- Will informing the product/service provider and possibly receiving compensation for my complaint be worth my efforts? If the answer to this question is "yes", then a letter or phone call is appropriate.

2. A COMPLAINT LETTER OR A TELEPHONE CALL

Complaint letters are generally the best choice for larger complaints (complaints involving products/services over $20 in value). They also are appropriate when certain evidence must be provided, such as a picture, a receipt, or any other necessary items.

Phone calls are commonly used for small complaints (complaints involving products/services less than $20 in value or complaints needing immediate attention).

3. ESSENTIAL RULE

When voicing a complaint, you should maintain a mature and professional attitude. No matter how justified your complaint is, avoid making the representative of the company an enemy. In many cases, the person with whom you are speaking is not the person responsible for causing your problem. Having this person work for you, rather than against you, will result in the best conclusion.

4. CONTACTING THE CORRECT PERSON

Determining who to communicate your complaint to is essential for a quick and effective resolution. To determine who handles complaints may be as simple as a telephone call to the company and inquiring to whom complaints are to be sent. Furthermore, telephone numbers or addresses are usually located on the back of product packaging, on receipts, or contained within the warranty information. Company telephone numbers can also be obtained by calling toll free information (for additional information on toll-free telephone numbers, refer to the "Telecommunication" section on page 106). Finally, many companies maintain web-sites, which may include contact information for customer service.

5. GATHERING EVIDENCE

Your complaint will be most effective if you take the time to gather sufficient evidence. In some cases, this evidence may be as simple as a defective product or several pictures of a poor paint job. However, other cases may require more information. The key is to collect as much evidence as possible. Evidence includes the following:
- Names and titles of people who provided you defective services.
- The date and time the defective service was rendered.

- Receipts to document the purchase.
- Previous correspondence (*Be sure to only send copies and retain the originals in your records).
- Pictures that are directly relevant to your complaint.
- Any other form of evidence that is relevant to your complaint.

6. DETERMINING COMPENSATION

Before writing a complaint letter or making a complaint telephone call, you need to determine what compensation you are seeking. This involves detailing why the product/service does not meet your expectations and determining a reasonable method to resolve your complaint. Compensation can come in many different forms including replacing a certain dollar amount, providing a discount on your next purchase, or having the service provided again.

The key to obtaining a resolution to your complaint is to be reasonable. This includes being reasonable as to the type and amount of compensation you expect as well as the time frame in which you expect the compensation.

7. FORMATING A COMPLAINT LETTER & TELEPHONE CALL

1. Identify the reason why you are writing early in the letter or conversation. State that you have a complaint and you are requesting compensation. Do not provide all the details of your complaint in the first sentence.
2. Provide a full description of the problem you incurred including any evidence to support your complaint. However, keep the letter brief and to the point.
3. State the exact compensation you believe to be reasonable for the problem you incurred and explain why the compensation you requested is reasonable. Be sure to state the time frame that you want your request to be completed in.
4. State why it is in the company's best interest to grant you your request. Be sure to follow the "Essential Rule" - do not become threatening or try to imply that you believe the problem was deliberate.
5. Express confidence that you will be granted the compensation you requested.

6. Complete your letter or telephone conversation by providing the recipient with information where they can contact you (i.e. address, telephone number, and/or email address).
7. If sending a complaint letter, be sure to keep a copy of the letter for your records.

♦ For a sample complaint letter, see page 32.

8. WHEN THE INITIAL COMPLAINT DOES NOT WORK

Occasionally you may not receive a response or accomplish what you intended to from your initial complaint letter or telephone call. If this occurs, follow up with a letter, not a phone call, as a letter tends to be more effective. Follow these steps:

1. In the first paragraph, state your disappointment in the company's delayed response to your complaint.
2. Make two copies of the letter. Send one to the person you previously contacted and the other to the President, Chief Executive Officer (C.E.O.), or owner of the company. Be sure to inform each recipient who else is also receiving that letter.
3. Send a copy of your first letter as proof of your initial attempt to inform the company of your complaint. If you originally made a telephone call, refer to the telephone call in your letter, including the date the call was made, who you spoke with, and the details of the discussion.
4. State that you would like immediate attention directed to your complaint.
5. Be sure to provide information where you can be contacted.

♦ For a sample of a "no response" complaint letter, see page 33.

COMPLAINT LETTER

Problem Company Inc.   Upset Customer
Attn: Ms. Big Boss, Customer Service Director   321 Fix It Rd.
123 Broken Down Rd.   Very Cool, State 33333
Slow, State 33334

January 1, 2005

Dear Ms. Boss,

I am writing to inform you of the defective widget I purchased from your Slow, State store location last week, and to request that a new widget be sent to me immediately, as well as additional compensation for my time and postage expense.

On December 24, 2004, I purchased your newest widget (which has been sent with this letter), as a Christmas present for my parents (see attached copy of receipt). As you can imagine, I was quite embarrassed on Christmas morning when the widget I purchased from your store failed to work properly for my parents. To make matters worse, when I tried to exchange the broken widget for a properly working widget on December 26, your store manager, Mr. Jim Glow, stated that your company, under any circumstance, would not allow cash refunds or exchanges for opened widgets.

As a frequent purchaser of widgets from your store, I understand that it is rare for a widget to malfunction. I also understand that Mr. Glow is fairly new to your organization and is unaware of the amount of widgets that I purchase from your store every year. However, your company's policy disallowing a customer to return a malfunctioning widget for a properly working widget is a bad policy.

I request that you replace the malfunctioning widget I have sent with this letter. I also request that you provide me with a store certificate as compensation of my time and the postage expense I incurred in order to mail you the malfunctioning widget.

I am sure that you understand the importance of my continued widget purchases from your store and that you will take the necessary steps to resolve this issue by January 20, 2005. Please have all materials mailed to my home (address is provided above). If needed, you may also contact me by telephone at (111)111-1111 to discuss this matter further.

Sincerely,

Upset Customer

"NO RESPONSE" COMPLAINT LETTER

Problem Company Inc.   Upset Customer
Attn: Ms. Big Boss, Customer Service Director   321 Fix It Rd.
Attn: Mr. Head Honcho, President   Very Cool, State 33333
123 Broken Down Rd.
Slow, State 33334

January 21, 2005

Dear Ms. Boss,

I am writing to express my disappointment in your failure to address the complaint letter I addressed to you, dated January 1, 2005. I have attached a copy of that letter for you to refer to. In addition, I have sent a copy of my original letter, as well as this letter, to Mr. Head Honcho, President of Problem Company, Inc., in hopes of receiving an immediate response from your company.

As a frequent customer of the Problem Company, Inc. store in Slow, State, I find it difficult to understand why I have not received a response to my original complaint. I suggest that immediate attention be given to this letter and my original complaint. If I fail to receive a response from your company by February 15, 2005, I will have no option but to take my future widget business to No-Problems Company, Inc.

Please have all materials mailed to my home (address is provided above). If needed, you may also contact me by telephone at (111)111-1111 to discuss this problem further.

If you have already responded to my concerns, please disregard this letter.

Sincerely,

Upset Customer

CREDIT CARDS

This section will provide insight into the use of credit cards, such as what some of the benefits of credit cards are, what credit cards should be used, and how to avoid getting into and staying out of debt. In addition, this section will provide you with some suggestions on negotiating better terms with your credit card company.

1. BENEFITS OF CREDIT CARDS

Credit cards provide a number of benefits. However, some credit cards are more beneficial than others. Listed below are the primary benefits credit cards can provide.

Security

Credit cards provide the user a method of payment when cash is unavailable and personal checks can not be used. For example, when travelling you may have an occasion to use them, such as when your car breaks down, where you have insufficient cash and personal checks are not accepted. In this situation, having a credit card enables you to make your payment.

Establishing Credit

Establishing credit, particularly for young adults, is difficult but important. Receiving credit from a major credit card company and properly using it are great ways to establish your credit history. Establishing a good credit history will allow you to receive important loans later in life, for example, when applying for a loan to purchase a new car or home.

Flexibility

Credit cards provide the user flexibility in their budget. When properly used, a credit card can provide the user forty-five (45) days or more of free credit. Consider the example on the following page.

Example: Your credit card has a billing date of 5th of every month. Payment for that credit card is to be received by the 15th of every month. Therefore, if you make a purchase on the 6th, that purchase will not show up until the following month and will not be due until the 15th of that month. Assuming that you pay off the balance of that purchase on time, you have just been provided use of that credit card company's money for almost 45 days with no interest or fees.

2. WHAT CREDIT CARD SHOULD YOU USE?

Determining what credit card to apply for and use should be based on the benefits you receive for using it and at what expense you must pay for using it. Listed below are a few suggestions to consider when deciding what credit card to use and how to minimize your expense.

Annual Fees

Some credit cards charge an annual fee. Frequently, these are credit cards that are offering valuable benefits to their customers, such as frequent flier mileage or insurance coverage on purchases. Unless you use your credit card frequently and charge large amounts, such as for business purposes, there are other credit cards to choose from that do not charge an annual fee and provide excellent benefits.

Interest Rates

In many instances, the credit cards offering the best promotions, such as cash back or free gifts, also charge the highest interest rates. Therefore, as long as you can pay off your monthly balance each month, interest rates are not that important. However, if you know you will be carrying a monthly balance, watch for the best interest rates.

Insurance

Many credit card companies are offering customers insurance coverage on purchases made with the company's credit card. The details and specifics of this coverage vary from credit card company to credit card company. Therefore, contact credit card companies you are considering and ask them to provide you details and examples of how the insurance coverage works.

Free Stuff

Credit card companies offer customers a variety of promotions, many of which include free stuff, including T-shirts, movie tickets, gasoline, and even air travel. Before signing up for a card that is offering a promotional item you want, be sure to pay particular attention to the details of the card, such as the interest rate, annual fees, and what you need to do in order to earn the free stuff. In many cases, just purchasing the free item would be cheaper and easier than jumping through a number of hoops and paying various fees in order to get the item free.

3. CREDIT CARD DEBT

Credit Cards offer a number of benefits for stringent users. However, credit cards offer many more negatives to the majority of credit card users. Because of the easy access to credit and lack of budgeting, some credit card users find themselves living far above their means. Below are various suggestions to implement in order to stay out of credit card debt and for getting out of credit card debt.

Keep One Card

Most people have a need for only one credit card. Therefore, find a credit card that offers a number of advantages and cancel any other cards you have.

Balance Due Card

To keep from going into credit card debt, apply for a credit card that requires the entire balance to be paid off each month.

Establish A Credit Limit

If you have a problem purchasing too many items on your credit card each month, but just are unwilling to get rid of your card, contact your credit card company and request your available credit be reduced to an amount you are able to pay off every month.

Consolidate Balances

If you have several credit cards with balances, find the credit card with the lowest interest rate and consolidate your other credit card balances to that card. This will enable you to see your complete debt on one statement and the progress you make in paying the balance off.

Reduce The Interest Rate

If you are carrying a balance, or are considering consolidating other credit card balances to one card, contact the credit card company you are considering consolidating the cards to and negotiate for a better interest rate. When negotiating, simply state that you want to consolidate your other credit card balances and wish to consolidate them with their company. Ask to have a special interest rate applied to the consolidated amount. If they hesitate in offering you a special interest rate, suggest you will use another company.

Keep A Journal
One of the problems with credit cards is that customers are unaware of their credit card balance until the statement arrives each month. By keeping a journal of your monthly credit card purchases, you will be aware of the exact balance on your card.

Stop Using Credit
In order to pay off your debts, you need to stop using your credit card. The most effective method to stop using your card to purchase items is to cut up your card. If you encounter an emergency where you need to use the card, you can contact the credit card company by telephone to have a purchase credited to your account.

Budget Monthly Payments
To assist in paying off your credit card debt, create a budget. (Read the "Budgeting" section on page 11 to determine how to make a budget work for you.) Designate a specific amount in your budget to be used toward paying off the balance of your credit card each month.

Avoid Late Fees/Bad Credit
Late fees can be obtained two ways: not making your monthly payment on time or paying less than the minimum amount. In addition to being expensive, late fees are also a sign of bad credit and will show up on your credit report. To avoid these fees, contact your credit card company. Inform them of your financial situation and request assistance. The most common assistance will include changing your billing period so that your payment due date will occur at a more convenient time or lowering your monthly minimum. Lowering your monthly payment will cause your balance to be paid off over a longer amount of time and increase the amount of interest you will have to pay, but it will keep your credit history clean until you are able to make additional contributions toward the balance.

CREDIT REPORT

Credit reports are used by a number of organizations, such as potential creditors, employers, and landlords. The information is provided as a service to these organizations so that they are aware of the financial risk (possible default) you present to them. Therefore, understanding and ensuring that the information in your credit report is accurate and complete is very important. Provided in this section is a list of your rights under the Fair Credit Reporting Act (FCRA) and information on how to request a credit report.

1. YOUR RIGHTS
The FCRA was established to provide accuracy, fairness, and privacy of information in the files of consumer reporting agencies. These agencies are credit bureaus that gather and sell information about you, such as if you pay your bills on time, if you have filed for bankruptcy, and how much credit you are eligible for. In addition, the FCRA provides the individual specific rights regarding the information contained within credit reports. These rights include the following:

Who Uses Information Against You?
Anyone who uses information gathered from a credit report to take action against you, such as denying you credit or employment, must provide you with the name, address, and telephone number of the credit reporting agency that provided them the information they used as the basis for their action.

Disputing Inaccurate Information

If you believe information listed in your credit report is inaccurate, you can dispute the information. First, contact the credit reporting agency about your dispute. The credit reporting agency must investigate the items within 30 days by presenting to its information source all relevant evidence you submit, unless your dispute is frivolous. The source must review your evidence and report its findings to the credit reporting agency. If the source was in error, the source must also advise other national credit reporting agencies to which it has provided data of any error. The credit reporting agency must then provide you a written report of the investigation and a report if the investigation results in a change.

If the investigation does not resolve the dispute, you can add a brief statement to your file for organizations requesting to see your information. In addition, if the information in dispute is deleted or a statement is filed, it is your responsibility to request that anyone who has recently received your report be notified of the changes. Any inaccurate information that has been corrected or deleted on your credit report will be made within 30 days after the investigation is complete.

Length Of Reporting Time

A credit reporting agency can not report negative information that is more than seven years old. Bankruptcies can be reported for up to ten years.

Limited Access To Files

A credit reporting agency can only report information about you to people or organizations recognized by the FCRA. The most common people or organizations that have access to your information are creditors, insurers, employers, and landlords. In addition, anyone you give written approval to can access your credit report.

2. AVOIDING CREDIT & INSURANCE OFFERS

Creditors and insurers may use file information as the basis for sending you unsolicited offers of credit or insurance. Such offers must include a toll-free telephone number for you to call if you want your name and address removed from future lists.

If you request to have your name and address removed by telephone, you must be kept off the list for two years. However, if you request, complete, and return the credit reporting agency's form provided for this purpose, you must be kept off the list indefinitely.

3. REQUESTING A CREDIT REPORT

A credit reporting agency should give you the information in your file and a list of everyone that has requested it recently. The fee for this service can be up to $8; however it can be provided at no charge if you meet one of the following conditions:

- A person/organization has taken action against you because of information supplied by the credit-reporting agency, and you request the report within 60 days of receiving notice of the action.
- You are unemployed and plan to seek employment within 60 days.
- You are on welfare.
- Your report is inaccurate due to fraud.

4. LOCATING A CREDIT REPORTING AGENCY

There are numerous credit reporting agencies available. Many provide their users specific information; however, some do provide an overall credit report. To locate one or more credit reporting agencies that meet your specific requirements, use a search engine on the Internet, contact a local bank or financial institution, or contact the state or federal consumer protection agency.

EDUCATION LOANS

One thing that many college graduates have in common is education loans. Although education loans are helpful while in school, having to pay them back when you are finished with school can be quite a burden. To help minimize this burden, this section will describe several methods you can implement in order to save yourself some money while paying back your loans. The larger the loan and the longer the repayment period, the more significant these savings will be.

1. PAY YOUR LOAN ON TIME

Some lenders will offer credits or interest rate reductions for timely payments. Most often, if this service is available, you will receive your first credit/interest rate reduction after the twelfth payment. Credits/interest rate reductions after this point may occur less frequently. However, if you can get a credit/interest rate reduction on your loan by simply making your payment on time then, by all means, make your payments on time. In addition, paying your student loans on time will assist you in establishing a good credit record.

2. DIFFICULTY PAYING YOUR LOANS

If you are having difficulty making your loan payments each month, contact your lender immediately. Inform them of the reason you are unable to make your payments. Your lender will often work with you to develop a program that will meet your financial situation. Although this is not a direct way to save money, it will assist in keeping your credit report clean and providing you the ability to finance future loans without difficulty.

3. CONSOLIDATE YOUR LOANS

If you have loans with more than one company, consider consolidating them. This will offer you several benefits, such as less paperwork, a reduction in the writing and mailing of checks, and a possible reduction in your total monthly payment.

When consolidating your loans, you may be increasing the time frame for repaying your loan. Therefore, the total amount of interest paid on the loan is increased. In addition, loan companies may charge fees if you decide to consolidate your loan with another company.

4. PREPAY YOUR LOAN

If you have the funds available, consider paying off your student educational loan early. Although it may be tempting to use your extra funds for more entertaining things, making an extra payment can save you a considerable amount in accumulated interest.

5. ELECTRONIC PAYMENTS

Several lenders offer the ability for educational loan payments to be made electronically. This service is a great benefit for the lender because it reduces their overall administrative costs. Therefore, in order to have borrowers make their payments using this method, some lenders provide the incentive of reduced interest rates. This is an excellent method to save a considerable amount of money, particularly if you are making payments on a large loan. You will also save the time and expense of writing and mailing checks every month. Finally, by paying electronically you will avoid being charged late fees.

6. TAX DEDUCTIONS

Qualifying individuals may claim deductions for interest accumulated on education loans. Because tax laws are constantly changing, be sure to consult with your tax accountant or contact the Internal Revenue Service to determine if you are eligible for these deductions.

EXTENDED WARRANTIES

Did you know that approximately only ten to twenty percent of extended warranties are actually used? Therefore, consider the following:

- Is what you are buying likely to need repairs?
- What is the value of your peace of mind for owning an extended warranty contract?

1. WARRANTY OPTIONS

Before purchasing, or not purchasing an extended warranty, inquire about any additional warranty options. Many sales people will offer only the most expensive extended warranty options because of correlated commissions.

2. READ THE FINE PRINT

Do not rely solely on the sales person's verbal explanation of the extended warranty. Actually obtain a copy of the warranty contract and read it carefully. Be sure to search for exclusions, limitations, or requirements that appear to be unreasonable. In addition, determine what company will ultimately be responsible for any repairs and/or maintenance.

3. DEDUCTIBLE WARRANTIES

Some extended warranty programs offer a deductible option. This option allows you to reduce the expense of the extended warranty, but may also increase your expense, depending on the amount of needed repairs.

4. DELAYED PURCHASE OF EXTENDED WARRANTIES

Many extended warranty contracts usually offer customers one year from the date of purchase to purchase an extended warranty. Therefore, confirm the time frame available for sign-up for the extended warranty program when purchasing products as prices for these programs tend to rise sharply after the grace period has expired.

5. CASH LAYOUT WARRANTIES

Try to avoid extended warranties in which you have to pay for the cost of the repairs and then be reimbursed by the warranty provider. This simply allows the company to use your money for an extended period of time, while you accept the burden of a broken product and money out-of-hand.

6. UNKNOWN CANCELLATIONS

After you purchase an extended warranty, be careful not to void the extended warranty contract. For example, some extended warranties on automobiles require that all maintenance on the vehicle be performed by one of their certified mechanics. In addition, some automobile extended warranties for electronic problems are voided if you allow a company other than the dealer to install an automobile alarm.

7. TRANSFERRING WARRANTIES

An advantage of some extended warranties is the ability to transfer the warranty of a product. This is a great benefit when attempting to sell a high-valued item, such as an automobile.

8. CANCELING WARRANTIES

Once you purchase an extended warranty, you are usually given from thirty to sixty days to cancel your contract and receive a full refund. Other companies will offer a pro-rata refund for the cancellation of an extended warranty based on the time period that the contract was in place. However, these companies may also charge you an administrative fee for processing your extended warranty.

FLEXIBLE SPENDING ACCOUNT

Many employers offer their employees comprehensive health and dental insurance. However, some health-related expenses may not be covered under your standard insurance (i.e. vision care, co-payments, and certain dental expenses). As a result, many employers offer flexible spending accounts, or health care expense accounts (HCEA), to assist with these expenses.

1. BENEFITS OF FLEXIBLE SPENDING
Money paid into a flexible spending account is considered a "pre-tax" expense. This means that funds designated to go into your flexible spending account are paid into that account prior to federal and state income taxes and social security taxes being withheld. Therefore, depending on which specific tax bracket you are in, you can save a considerable amount of money by using a flexible spending account.

2. DRAWBACKS OF FLEXIBLE SPENDING
Although there are some negative aspects to a flexible spending account, it could still be worth the time and investment. Below are important factors to consider before participating in a flexible spending account.

Not All Expenses Are Covered
Beware! Not all uncovered health expenses are reimbursable by your flexible spending account. Therefore, before determining how much to contribute, it is important to review your specific flexible spending account for a list of which health expenses are covered and which are not. If you are unsure whether a particular item can be reimbursed, call your employer's human resource department or flexible spending account provider and ask them for assistance. When talking with someone regarding your flexible

spending account, be sure to keep notes on your conversation in case you encounter conflicting information at a later date. Your notes should include the name of the service agent, the date and time of your discussion, and the substance of that conversation.

Financial Limits
Employers may limit employee contributions to their flexible spending accounts. Nevertheless, some firms do allow employee contributions as high as $5,000 and as low as $10.

3. SUBMITTING A CLAIM
Be sure to submit your claims for health expenses reimbursable from your flexible spending account. Reimbursement procedures and forms can be obtained from your human resource department or the flexible spending provider. Delaying this procedure can increase the time you receive reimbursement, as well as the chances of loosing documentation needed for reimbursement.

4. HOW MUCH TO CONTRIBUTE
Determining how much to contribute to your flexible spending account is extremely important as any remaining funds in your account at the end of the year can not be recovered. Due to this penalty, it is highly recommended that you estimate your additional health care needs conservatively, such as services not covered by your standard health coverage. A chart has been provided below to assist you.

Health Coverage	Estimated Expense
Standard Health Plan Deductible/Co-pay	
Prescription Deductible/Co-pay	
Optical Care (exam, glasses, contacts)	
Dental Care (exam, corrective procedures)	
Periodic Clinic Visits (i.e. Allergy shots)	
Other:	
Other:	
Other:	
Total	

FOOD & DRINKS

Saving money on food does not have to include just eating potatoes, macaroni & cheese, and ramen noodles. There are numerous methods that can help you keep your food expenses down without giving up the variety and taste of your favorite foods.

1. GROCERY SAVING TECHNIQUES

The following techniques may help you reduce your grocery bill:

- Make a detailed grocery list prior to shopping and only purchase those items on your list.
- Avoid shopping on an empty stomach, as you may be tempted to purchase expensive, unnecessary snack foods.
- Shop alone, as children and/or friends can encourage impulse purchases.
- Shop at lower-priced warehouse grocery stores as upper-scale grocery stores usually charge a premium for their items.
- Avoid purchasing high-priced convenience items such as pre-cooked chicken or pre-chopped vegetables. Instead, do your own preparation.
- Collect, and use, coupons for items that you often use. Coupons can reduce your grocery expense significantly.
- Shop at stores that offer double or triple coupons. For example, if you use a coupon for $0.35 off a bag of potato chips, the store will actually deduct $0.70 off that price. Therefore, by simply using 5 coupons a week of at least $0.35 each, you will save at least $1.75 off your total grocery bill (or $84 per year).
- Consider purchasing store-brand or generic items. In many cases, there are only slight differences, such as packaging.

- Plan your meals and snacks ahead of time and shop on a weekly basis to avoid returning to the store. This will avoid impulse purchases and provide you more time to do other activities besides shopping for groceries.
- Avoid purchasing non-food items, such as cleaning materials, razors and paper products, from the supermarket because they usually have large mark-ups on these products to compensate for other lower priced items. Instead, purchase non-food items from warehouse clubs or discount department stores.
- Consider purchasing products on the bottom and top shelves, as cheaper products tend to be located in areas with less exposure.
- Establish a monthly/weekly grocery budget and stick to it (see the "Budgeting" section on page 11).
- As you shop, be aware of the price of the items you are purchasing. This is important for the following reasons:
  1. You will be aware of any over-charges made at the checkout counter.
  2. It will help you create a budget for groceries and become more efficient at comparison-shopping.
- Be aware of the prices other stores are advertising for items you frequently use. If another grocery store is having a big sale, it may be worth the $15 in savings to shop at that store that week.
- Check to make sure that you have all of your groceries prior to leaving the store.
- Review your receipt prior to leaving the store to ensure that you were properly charged, that your coupons were deducted, and that all advertised sale prices were honored.
- Count your change prior to leaving the store.

2. PACKING LUNCHES & SNACKS

Packing your own lunch and snacks is an easy way to save a significant amount of money. For example, if you purchased snacks (average cost of $1.30) three times a week while at work or when travelling and you purchased lunch everyday (average cost of $5), in one year you would have spent over $1,200 on snacks and lunch. Although certain careers and situations do not lend themselves to packing a lunch or snacks, there are many careers where this is an acceptable alternative to eating out. Listed below are suggestions to help you save money by packing your own lunch and snacks.

- If packing your lunch is not popular at your workplace, encourage others to pack their lunches and eat together. Also request that your employer invest in a refrigerator and microwave for the employees.
- Plan your lunches when doing your weekly grocery shopping. Purchase some of your favorite items and prepare them during the weekend for your convenience during the week. Below are some examples.
  1. Cut up fresh vegetables so that they are easily ready to pack in your lunch each day.
  2. Make larger quantities for dinner during the week and take the leftovers to lunch.
  3. Avoid purchasing convenience, quantity-size items as they are priced at a premium. Instead, invest in some reusable containers and purchase value-sized items.
  4. Be creative with packing your lunch so that you do not become bored or discouraged with bringing your lunch to work. To accomplish this, stroll the grocery store for ideas that you can incorporate into your lunch.
- Pack snacks for work. For example, bring store-bought sodas and pretzels to prevent visits to the vending machines.
- When traveling by car, pack a small cooler with beverages and snacks in order to avoid paying inflated prices for these items at convenience stores.
- When traveling by air, especially if you have lengthy layovers, pack snacks in your carry-on luggage to avoid purchasing expensive items from airport services.

3. EVERY DAY DINNERS

As an excuse for frequenting restaurants, people complain that they either do not know how to cook, or do not have the time to cook. There are several products available to make cooking fast, easy, and economical. Considering that an average dinner can cost anywhere from $8 to $20, a significant amount of money can be saved by following these suggestions.

- Purchase a few "Quick & Easy" cookbooks. These are usually conveniently located at the checkout line at your grocery store. The recipes generally make 4 to 6 servings and usually require purchasing 5 to 6 ingredients that are already prepared, such as canned vegetables and soup mixes. There are also recipes on common grocery items or in advertisements featuring items on sale that week.

- If you are not willing to try to cook, purchase pre-made meals in the frozen food section of the grocery store. Although they are more expensive than a meal you prepare yourself, they are significantly less expensive and often healthier than eating out.

4. DINING OUT

While dining out is fun and enjoyable, it can also be very expensive. Below are tips on saving money while dining out.

- Allot a certain dollar amount per week/month to dining out. (See the "Budgeting" section on page 11 for more information)
- Order take-out food from your favorite restaurant. You will save money on the drinks and the tip.
- Do not order more than you can eat. Or, if the helpings are large, ask for a "take-home" bag and eat the leftovers for lunch the next day.
- Avoid ordering both an appetizer and a dessert at the same meal. Or, if you do order a dessert, share.
- Avoid ordering alcoholic beverages.
- Join frequent-diner programs. These programs allow you to earn points that can be used toward free appetizers, entrees, and desserts for every dollar you spend at restaurants.
- Contact a local culinary school about public dinners. There are currently about 100 private cooking schools in the U.S. that offer gourmet meals prepared by students to the public. In a restaurant these meals would typically cost about $30 to $40 per person, but they are usually offered at a significant discount at the culinary school.
- Scan the newspaper, Internet, and flyers for coupons for your favorite restaurant. Many locations will have coupons offering free appetizers or "buy one – get one free" specials.
- Do not feel obliged to tip if the service was not satisfactory.

FREE PRODUCTS & DISCOUNTS

Every company that manufactures products would like additional customers. Therefore, in order to inform potential customers about their products, companies offer sample sizes and coupons for their products. In order to receive these samples and coupons follow these suggestions below.

1. TOLL-FREE TELEPHONE NUMBERS
Many companies, particularly national and international companies, offer toll-free telephone numbers. These telephone numbers are useful to voice complaints, as well as request free samples and/or coupons. Simply state that you are interested in using their product and would like to try a sample. The worst thing that can happen is that the customer service representative will say that there are no samples available. If you cannot locate a toll-free telephone number, call the 1-800 toll-free directory for assistance. For more information about using the toll-free directory, see the "Telecommunications" section on page 106.

2. COMPANY ADDRESSES
Almost all companies list their address on their products. If not, you can also find them on the Internet. When writing the company, simply write a short note stating that you would like to receive a free sample and some discount coupons. Also be sure to provide them your mailing address so the company can respond to your request.

3. INTERNET

Most companies can now be contacted through their web-site on the Internet. This is a great way to contact a company for free samples and discounts because it is quick and easy. In addition, companies also provide on-line coupons that can be printed directly from their web-site.

Besides companies offering free samples and discounts on their own products, many independent web-sites are now dedicated to offering free samples and discounts for various companies all in one convenient location. These web-sites usually require you to provide them with some basic information about yourself. The information that you enter is collected and analyzed to determine marketing strategies based on your individual demographics.

In order to locate these web sites, simply use any of the various Internet search engines available and enter the words "coupons", "free stuff", and "free coupons" in the search field.

HEALTH INSURANCE

Having proper health insurance coverage for yourself and your family is essential. Without proper coverage, you, or one of your family members, are at risk of becoming injured or ill, at risk of loosing any money you have saved, and at risk of becoming permanently disabled with no ability to finance any future health care needs. Finding adequate health insurance coverage can be confusing, but by reviewing the following section, you will be able to better understand, and optimize, your health insurance options immediately after graduation and beyond.

1. COVERAGE BETWEEN GRADUATION & EMPLOYMENT

Although some health insurance programs begin on your first day of employment, many employer's plans do not take effect until at least 90 days after employment begins, and in some cases, much longer. For most people, this means that from the date they graduate until their health insurance begins, they do not have any health insurance coverage. Fortunately, there are some health care options available during this period of time.

Parents' Health Plan

There are a few health plans that will provide insurance to dependents until they begin working after graduating from college. Therefore, be sure to have your parent(s) check their health insurance policy for coverage of recent college graduates. If you are not covered, ask if your parent's health plan offers recent graduates the ability to extend health insurance coverage through the Consolidated Omnibus Budget Reconciliation Act (COBRA). COBRA is a federal program developed to provide a bridge between health plans for qualified workers, their spouses, and their dependent children when their health insurance might otherwise be cut off. However, you should be aware that this option tends to be fairly expensive.

School's Health Plan

Most school health programs offer their students an annual health plan while attending school. These plans are sometimes annual policies and may not expire until several months after graduation. In addition, some schools will allow their students to purchase extensions of the school's health coverage after graduation and may even possibly offer a COBRA program.

Short Term Medical Insurance

If no other options are available, you may need to consider purchasing a short-term medical insurance plan. Unlike group plans, where the costs and risks associated with health care are distributed among many people, individual health policies are written to take into account your own personal health history. Because of the structure of this type of program, it tends to be one of the most expensive health insurance options. Some facts to know about short-term medical insurance include the following items:

- Coverage is for a limited period of time (typically 1 month to 6 months)
- Typically does not cover pre-existing conditions
- Specially designed to cover unexpected events
- Typically does not cover preventive care, physicals, immunizations, dental, or vision care
- Discounts may be available through your schools Alumni Association or other organization

2. HEALTH INSURANCE PLANS

At your new job, you may be extended the opportunity to participate in your employer's health insurance plan. In some cases, employers will have only one health care option available. However, some employers, offer their employees numerous choices. Whatever your situation, this section was developed to help you better understand the choice of health care options you are provided.

Managed Care Plans

Managed Care Plans were developed to provide a health care delivery program that controls cost through the coordination and arrangement of health services. Because of the nature of these plans, they tend to be the most economical. However, in some cases, your options for care are limited.

- **Health Maintenance Organizations (HMO)**
  HMOs are a managed care plan that provides health care through a network of doctors, hospitals and medical professionals. Participants and/or their employers pay a monthly premium in exchange for the HMO to provide comprehensive care. Generally, participants cannot seek care from physicians outside of the plan's network unless they are willing to pay for the service themselves. The only way participants can visit an outside physician, and have the expense covered by their insurance, is to have their HMO approve the visit.

  Advantages
  - No deductibles
  - Low premiums
  - Low out-of-pocket costs
  - Comprehensive benefits
  - Minimal paperwork
  - HMOs focus on wellness and preventive care (office visits, immunizations, physicals, etc.)

  Disadvantages
  - You must choose a Primary Care Physician
  - You are restricted in the amount of physicians from which you can select
  - You must receive a referral from your Primary Care Physician in order to have a visit to a specialist covered by the HMO

- **Point of Service (POS)**
  POS is a managed care plan that allows members to see providers outside of the network, usually at a slightly higher co-payment or deductible cost. Although a POS plan is more flexible than an HMO, it also requires participants to select a Primary Care Physician.

  Advantages
  - No deductible
  - Out-of-pocket costs are limited
  - Smaller co-payments
  - Ability to visit non-network physicians

Disadvantages
- Must select a Primary Care Physician
- Considerable co-payments or deductibles for non-network care

- **Preferred Provider Organizations (PPO)**
  PPOs are a managed care plan that is considerably different than an HMO. The largest difference is that you do not need to designate a Primary Care Physician and you can visit Specialists at any time without referrals. In general, for a managed care plan, PPOs are the most flexible, but that flexibility may come at a higher cost to you.

Advantages
- Choice of health care providers
- Financial incentives are available if you visit physicians from the plans preferred provider network
- Access to visit any specialist

Disadvantages
- May have to deal with reimbursement claim forms and other paperwork
- May have to pay a deductible
- Premiums are higher than those of an HMO, but less than an indemnity plan

Indemnity Plans (Fee-For-Service or Reimbursement Plans)
Unlike the managed care plans, indemnity plans offer an incredible amount of flexibility. For example, participants can select any physician and/or hospital in any part of the country. However, this flexibility comes at a cost, such as higher premiums and out-of-pocket expenses. Yet, because of these high costs and the popularity of PPOs, indemnity plans are rarely provided to employees.

Advantages
- Select any desired hospital or physician
- Visit a specialist without obtaining permission

Disadvantages
- High premiums
- A deductible usually has to be satisfied prior to the plan beginning to pay claims. However, once the deductible is met, the plan typically pays 80% of the bill, while the member pays the remaining 20%.
- Some plans do not include preventive care as part of the program, such as physicals.
- Indemnity plans typically only pay for Usual, Reasonable and Customary (UCR) medical expenses. Therefore, if your physician charges higher fees for their services, you are responsible for the difference.

3. COMPARING HEALTH INSURANCE PLANS

As mentioned earlier in this section, some employers only offer their employees one choice of health coverage. However, some employers, offer their employees a number of options to choose from. This section is designed to help those with several health care options choose the plan best suited for them.

Service & Fee Checklist

In order to evaluate different health insurance plans, use the checklist provided on page 58. Information to complete this checklist can be obtained from your employer's human resource office or by contacting the insurance company directly.

	Health Plan #1	Health Plan #2	Health Plan #3
Services			

List the services that you need or want, such as dental and eye exams, regular physicals, family planning, coverage for emergency hospital care, choice of physician, and ability to see a specialist. Place a check by the plans that offer these services as part of their program.

	Health Plan #1	Health Plan #2	Health Plan #3
	_____	_____	_____
	_____	_____	_____
	_____	_____	_____
	_____	_____	_____
	_____	_____	_____
	_____	_____	_____
	_____	_____	_____
	_____	_____	_____
	_____	_____	_____
	_____	_____	_____
	_____	_____	_____

Fees

List the dollar value for services you expect to utilize

	Health Plan #1	Health Plan #2	Health Plan #3
Monthly/Annual Premium	_____	_____	_____
Medical Deductible/Co-pay (For Dr./Hospital visits)	_____	_____	_____
Prescription Deductible/Co-pay	_____	_____	_____
Fee for using services outside of the plan's network	_____	_____	_____
Other Fees	_____	_____	_____
Other Fees	_____	_____	_____
Other Fees	_____	_____	_____
Other Fees	_____	_____	_____
Totals	_____	_____	_____

As you begin to limit your choice of health insurance plans from the chart above, some plans may start to look similar. Before making your final decision, be sure to consider some of these items.

- What physicians, hospitals and specialists are included in the plan?
- Are there plenty of physicians to choose from?
- How difficult is it to obtain an appointment with a physician?
- Does the physician offer appointment times that match your needs?
- Are the physical offices conveniently located?
- How does the health plan handle out-of-town health needs?
- If you travel internationally, what kind of care does the plan offer?

4. LOCATING & SELECTING A PHYSICIAN

A health insurance plan is only as good as the physicians that provide care for that plan. Therefore, selecting the best physician for your needs is as important as selecting the best health insurance plan. This section will provide you some tips on how to find the best physician for your needs.

Locating a Physician

Most health insurance plans offer a directory of physicians. Physicians are often listed in categories, such as family care, general practitioner and specialist. In addition, they may list the limitations and/or special services that physician offers, such as the languages spoken and the age of patients accepted. These directories may be offered in both print and web-based versions. Be sure to ask for the latest version as participating physicians do change.

Selecting a Physician

Often, the best resource for selecting a physician is by word-of-mouth. Therefore, ask friends, family and co-workers who their physician is and what they think about the physician's services. If this is not an option, you will need to do your own process of selection. Listed below are some tips to help you select a physician.

- Locate all the physicians that offer the services you need and that are conveniently located to you.
- Contact them by telephone to determine if they are accepting new patients. Many times, physicians will limit the number of patients they will accept from a particular health insurance plan.
- Is the physician board certified? Contact your health insurance company about how to obtain this information.
- What is the physician's training (Medical School, Residency Program, etc.) and experience?
- Have complaints been registered or disciplinary action been taken against your physician? Contact your health insurance company about how to obtain this information.

5. MAXIMIZING YOUR HEALTH INSURANCE PLAN

For most people, health insurance is only something you use when you are sick or hurt. This is not the case. Most plans offer participants a number of services, including regular physicals, exams and education programs. You are paying for these services whether you use them or not. Therefore, you might as well use them. Listed below are some tips to get the most from your health insurance plan.

- When you sign-up with a health insurance plan, you will be provided a handbook of the plan. Review the handbook and be sure you completely understand all the benefits, coverage and limits of the plan.
- Many health insurance plans provide participants a monthly newsletter. Be sure to read these for helpful information, such as education programs and policy changes.
- Take advantage of regular health checkups
- When you visit your physician, ask lots of questions. Remember you are paying for this time, so make the most of it.
- Request information about discount prescription plans, such as mail-in orders for frequently used drugs.

6. HEALTH INSURANCE TERMS

Sometimes it may seem like health insurance companies have developed a new language to confuse their participants. To assist you in understanding your health insurance plan, listed below are some of the more commonly used terms in the health insurance industry.

Co-Insurance: The portion of health services the participant is responsible for. This is usually on an 80% covered, 20% non-covered basis.

Co-Payment: A fixed amount participants pay each time they visit a health plan provider and receive service. The common range is $5 to $25.

Covered Service: Those health care services that the health insurance plan is obligated to provide a participant based on the service contract between the participant and the health plan. If a service is not a covered service, it is the responsibility of the patient to pay for these services.

Deductible: A fixed amount the participant must pay each year before the insurer will begin covering health expenses of covered services.

Exclusions: Specific conditions or circumstances for which the health plan will not provide benefits.

Gatekeeper: Some HMOs consider the Primary Care Physician to be the "gatekeeper" who serves as the patient's initial contact and approval point for medical care and referrals.

Health Plan: Also known as health insurance, managed care plan, or third-party payor. These terms all refer to an organization or company that is liable to pay for the covered services provided to its participants.

Identification Card: A card certifying a participant is enrolled in a specific health plan and eligible for the benefits of that plan. This card is usually requested when visiting your physician or specialists that you have been referred to.

Maximum Out-of-Pocket: The most money that you will be required to pay annually for deductibles and coinsurance. This is a stated dollar amount set by the health plan, in addition to regular premiums.

Medically Necessary Services: Covered services required to preserve and maintain the health status of a member based on established medical practice standards. A health plan or part of the prior authorization process may decline to approve a service on the grounds it is not medically necessary.

Network: The doctors, clinics, health centers, medical group practices, hospitals, and other providers that an HMO, PPO, or other managed care plan has selected and contracted with to care for its participants.

Open Access: When a member is allowed to visit a specialist without a referral or prior authorization.

Participant/Member: Anyone enrolled in an HMO and entitled to receive benefits. This term is also used to describe a person covered by a particular health plan.

Preexisting Condition: A medical condition that is excluded from coverage by an insurance company, because the condition was believed to exist prior to the individual obtaining a policy from the particular insurance company.

Primary Care: Preventive health care and routine medical care that is typically provided by a doctor trained in internal medicine, pediatrics, or family medicine, or by a nurse, nurse practitioner, or physician's assistant.

Primary Care Physician (PCP): A provider who furnishes members with primary care. For many HMOs, the PCP is responsible for providing referrals and obtaining prior authorization for participants. The process varies by plan.

Prior Authorization (Pre-Authorization or Pre-Certification): Certain covered services require health plan authorization before service is rendered. These services vary by health plan and also the manner in which the prior authorization is obtained varies by health plan.

Provider: Medical professional (physician, nurse, dentist) or facility (hospital or clinic) that provides covered services in accordance with an agreement between the health plan and the provider.

Referral: The process by which one physician sends a member to another physician (usually a specialist) or to a hospital or diagnostic facility. The referral process varies greatly by health plan and type of service.

Specialist: A doctor or other health professional who's training and expertise are in a specific area of medicine, like cardiology or dermatology.

Usual, Reasonable and Customary (UCR): Most health plans will only pay a UCR fee for a particular medical service within a certain geographic region. Any amount above a UCR the participant is expected to pay. To avoid this situation, a participant should inquire to their physician about accepting the health plan's payment as a payment in full.

HOME FURNISHINGS

Furnishing a home can be very exciting, but it can also be quite expensive. This section will provide suggestions on how to furnish your home with quality furniture and still maintain a reasonable budget.

1. WHAT TO BUY

Furnishing your entire home at once would be ideal; however, for most people, furnishing a complete home is not a viable option. Therefore, before heading out to purchase furniture, determine what furnishings you believe are needed. For example, if you like to have friends over to your home very often, purchasing some couches, chairs, and a table may be more important than purchasing a bedroom dresser or pictures for the walls. Once you have a list of your priority furniture, start saving your money and be on the lookout for the best deals.

2. WHERE TO LOOK

There are numerous locations and methods to find great deals on home furnishings. Listed below are some suggestions to use.

Friends, Family, & Co-Workers

Ask your friends, family, and co-workers if they are aware of anyone or anyplace that would have the furnishings you are looking for. You may be surprised at the amount of furnishings that may be given to you either because someone is moving or because someone wants to get new furnishings and needs a place to get rid of their old furnishings.

Yard & Estate Sales/Thrift Shops

Yard and estate sales, as well as thrift shops, are great locations to find deals on home furnishings. You can find anything from bookshelves to pictures at these locations and often for great prices.

Rent-To-Own Stores

In most cases, rent-to-own stores should not be utilized for their rent-to-own business, as this can be a very expensive method to purchase furnishings. Instead, visit these locations for their previously rented furnishings that are available for purchase. These locations will usually offer these previously rented furnishings for significant discounts in order to make room for additional furnishings. However, before purchasing, look over the item very carefully as many of these locations have an "As-Is" policy.

Discount Furniture Stores

If you are a little leery about taking or purchasing furniture that has been used by someone else, consider shopping at a discount furniture store. Furniture is now being sold through national wholesale stores. Simply search the Internet or yellow pages for a location near you.

Furniture Manufacturers

If you are looking for better quality furniture, but do not want to pay the prices offered from the furniture stores in your area, consider purchasing furniture directly from the manufacturer.

There are a number of manufacturers that offer locations for customers to purchase furniture directly from them. Simply search the furniture stores in your area and find the names of manufacturers and model numbers of furniture you prefer. (Note that many furniture stores place new labels on furniture to stop customers from purchasing directly from the manufacturer, so you may have to work to find the correct name and model number of certain furniture.) Next, contact the manufacturer directly and ask if they sell items directly to the public. If they do, ask if they sell the specific name and model number of furniture you prefer and what they charge for shipping. If the manufacturer's location is close enough, it may be worth the time and money of renting a truck and shipping the furniture on your own.

3. HOW MUCH TO SPEND

Determining how much money you have to spend on home furnishings is an important step to purchasing furniture. A detailed section on how to determine this amount can be found in the "Budgeting" section on page 11.

HOTELS

Lodging prices tend to be considerably inflated. However, by using the methods discussed below, you should be able to obtain the lowest possible rate available.

1. BOOKING YOUR ROOM

Contact both the hotel's toll-free reservation center and the hotel directly, particularly with national chains, before making a reservation. These telephone numbers allow you to speak with two different people at two different locations, thus increasing the chance of price differentiation. In addition, try calling these locations again at different times of the day. Be sure to collect all the information about the hotel quotes, in addition to the person's name that is providing you the quote, in order to refer back to them as needed.

Also book your room as far in advance as possible to avoid higher prices due to a low availability of rooms. If you book your room in advance, re-check the current prices on occasion to determine if any discounts are being offered. When doing so, act as though you are a new customer.

2. DISCOUNTS

If you do not have the time or energy to contact hotels for discount rates, consider some of the following suggestions.

- Join as many hotel frequent-stay programs as possible. The majority of these programs are free of charge, and they offer a variety of benefits, such as free room-upgrades and frequent-flier miles.

- When you arrive for check-in, always ask if there are larger or better rooms available. If so, request a free upgrade, particularly if you are a member of the hotel's frequent-stay program.
- Ask for the following discounts or specials:
  1. Corporate, Association, Group, or Frequent-Flier Discounts
  2. Multi-night stay discount
  3. Weekend special
  4. Super-saver specials, such as summer specials
  5. Bed-and-breakfast rate (breakfast is offered in addition to the room's standard rate)
- Request these room options for possible discounts:
  1. Request a ground-level room, as many hotels offer discounts for these rooms.
  2. Request a room without a view.
  3. Request a smaller room.
- Coupons for hotels can be found when driving on various interstates across the country at restaurants, gas stations, and rest areas.
- For weekend stays, consider staying at hotels that are primarily used by business travelers during the week, such as downtown or airport hotels. These locations may offer discounts during the weekend.

3. OTHER CONSIDERATIONS

In most situations, choosing a hotel room primarily on price may not be the wisest decision. Listed below are other factors to consider when choosing where to stay.

- When considering two similarly priced hotels, consider the amenities, such as free continental breakfast, swimming pool/hot tub, and free parking.
- In most cases, taxes are not included in your quoted room rate. Be sure to inquire about this tax rate, as many areas have a special "hotel tax" which is higher than the normal sales tax.
- Avoid staying at a hotel during holidays. Since there is higher demand for rooms during the holidays, hotels will charge higher rates for rooms.

INVESTING

Investing can be very rewarding, but also confusing. However, investing is an extremely important concept and needs to be understood in order to build one's wealth.

This section provides a brief summary of factors to consider when investing in today's complex financial market. This material is intended for use as a reference for general investing information only. Before making any investment decision, you are encouraged to seek additional information. A list of additional resources has been provided on page 74.

1. BEFORE YOU INVEST
Before you begin investing, you need to have a complete understanding of your financial situation. In addition, you need to be sure you establish financial goals and determine the time frame you want your goals to occur. The "Budgeting" section, located on page 11, will assist you with this process.

2. INVESTING
Investing is a process that takes time and money. Below are factors to consider as you invest.

Start Early
The benefits of starting to invest early are tremendous, especially for long-term investments. By starting early, not only will your money have more opportunity to grow, but also, by starting early, saving a sufficient amount of money to meet your needs will be easier.

Risk Versus Reward

Be sure you understand that risk and reward go hand-in-hand. Lower risk (or low potential loss) investments will likely provide lower returns, whereas higher risk (or high potential loss) returns will likely obtain higher returns.

Make Investing A Habit

Determining the amount to invest will depend on your budget and available funds. By dedicating a specific amount to invest each month you will keep on track and will meeting your financial goals. This can be as simple as investing $100 a month into your savings account or more in-depth, such as investing a fixed amount monthly into a mutual fund.

Diversify

Diversifying is a process of minimizing your risk and maximizing your return with a proper balance (percentage weights) of different assets, such as cash, bonds, and stocks. Since no one-asset class consistently performs better than all others, a properly diversified portfolio will usually fluctuate less. The reasoning is based on the theory that losses from one asset class are offset by gains from other asset classes. The proper asset allocation is determined by a number of factors, such as age, financial goals, timeline, security, income, and the ability to accept risk. For more information about the diversity of assets that is best for you, refer to the "Additional Resource" section on page 74.

Evaluate Your Portfolio

Once you begin investing, you will need to create a financial portfolio (a listing of all your assets). This portfolio will be used to evaluate the productivity of your assets. By evaluating the productivity of your assets, you will be able to determine what steps you need to take, if any, to maximize the growth of your assets. This may involve selling or purchasing assets, or increasing the amount of investment into your portfolio. To ensure you are making the best decision, seek advice from professionals. Several resources are available in the "Additional Resource" section on page 74.

Taxes, Inflation And Fees

When making your investment decisions, taxes, inflation and fees need to be considered. Almost every form of investment is subject to tax. Therefore, be sure to know the tax consequences that apply to your investment. In addition, inflation should be considered. Inflation adjusts compared to the status of the economy. For example, say you have $1 in a savings account earning interest at a rate of two percent. If inflation is also rising at two percent, then that $1 is worth the same amount one year from now as it was when you put the $1 into the savings account. Therefore, if you wish that $1 to grow in value, place it in an account that is growing faster than the rate of inflation. Finally, fees for your investments need to be considered. For example, if you decide to invest in stocks, there are usually fees included in the purchase and the sale of those stocks.

3. INVESTMENT TYPES

The most common forms of investments are cash, bonds, stocks, and mutual funds. These are all discussed in the following pages.

Cash

Cash is one of the safest investment types to select from when developing an investment plan. However, cash investments, due to their low risk and high security, provide minimal growth.

The most common form of cash investment is an emergency fund. An emergency fund is money placed in a secure, but easily accessible account, for use during an emergency, such as a loss of employment or immediate health needs. The amount of funds placed into this account should be equal to three months of your normal expenses. A list of common cash investment accounts is listed below.

- **Savings Account**
  Savings accounts are usually offered by financial institutions, such as banks, and offer a very low rate of return. Money can usually be withdrawn without any penalty.
- **Certificates Of Deposit (CDs)**
  CDs are a specialized deposit that can be purchased from a financial institution, such as a bank or credit union. A CD is a loan you make to a financial institution over a certain time period. Most CDs provide annual interest payments during the life of the CD and will provide the original invested amount back when the CD expires.

  CDs often offer a higher rate of return than savings accounts because of the time requirement involved with a CD. However, you should be aware that if you withdraw money from a CD prior to its maturity, you most likely will be assessed a fee for early withdrawal.

- **Money Market Account**
  Money market accounts are invested primarily in short-term and high quality bonds, treasury bills, and CDs. They usually offer returns higher than a savings account, but lower than a CD. The advantage of money market accounts is the ability to withdraw money with no penalty. Some money market accounts are now insured up to a certain dollar amount. Therefore, prior to investing, determine if the money market account is insured and up to what limit.

Bonds

A bond is an IOU promised by the United States government (treasury bond, savings bonds), federal agencies, state and local governments (municipal bonds), and corporations (corporate bonds). In return for your loan, the creator of the bond promises to pay you a specified rate of interest during the life of the bond in addition to repaying the entire value of the bond when the time period is complete.

Bonds, just like other forms of investments, have several choices available to the investor. Based on the amount of risk the investor is willing to accept. The great thing about bonds is that a rating system has been developed to determine the amount of risk associated with a bond. A bond that is rated triple A (AAA) is usually safer than a bond that is rated double B (BB). However, the AAA bond will usually have a smaller rate of return than the BB bond. Bond ratings are available from several resources, such as the Internet, financial institutions, and newspapers. Below are descriptions of the various forms of bonds.

- **Treasury Bonds**
  The U.S. Treasury issues treasury notes (two to ten year maturity) and treasury bonds (ten to thirty year maturity). These investments are backed by the "full faith and credit" of the United States government and thus are considered low risk.
- **Municipal Bonds**
  Bonds issued by states and municipalities to finance public projects, such as roads, schools, and hospitals are municipal bonds. A benefit of municipal bonds is that they can be tax exempt from federal and state taxes.

- **Corporate Bonds**
  Occasionally corporations need to borrow money for long-term projects. Instead of issuing more shares of ownership (stock) to raise funds, a corporation will issue bonds. The risk associated with bonds will vary on the history and financial stability of the company offering the bond.

Stocks

A stock is a unit ownership in a corporation that you receive in the form of a piece of paper. The ownership of a stock entitles you to participate in various decision-making votes, such as the election of a company's directors or the sale of additional shares of company stock. By purchasing a share of ownership in the company, you are accepting the risk that the company's value may increase or decrease. This increase or decrease in value will be reflected in the company's stock price.

In addition to the increase or decrease in a company's stock price, some corporations offer their shareholders dividends. Dividends are payments of the company's profits that are not invested in the company. Dividends are most common in very large, low risk, and financially stable companies. Through dividend reinvestment plans (DRIP) – once you purchase stock in the company, many companies will allow you to purchase additional shares of the company's stock through the dividend payments. This gives you the ability to grow in the ownership of the company and avoid fees associated with purchasing additional shares.

Although there is no time frame associated with the length you must retain ownership of stock (except in specific situations), stock tends to be a long-term investment decision. In addition, the fees associated with the purchase and sale of shares of stock make frequent purchases and sales cost prohibitive.

Listed below are brief descriptions of the categories of company stocks.

- **Large-Cap Stocks**
  Stocks offered by large companies, such as automobile manufacturers and utility companies, are known as large-cap stocks or "blue chip" stocks. These shares generally have limited growth prospects, and investments in these companies are usually for long-term investment

horizons. Although the stock price may remain relatively stable, these companies will offer the largest dividends.

- **Mid-Cap Stocks**

  Stocks offered by mid-sized companies, such as regional grocery chains, are known as mid-cap stocks. These shares generally have good growth prospects and tend to re-invest profits. Therefore, dividends offered by these companies are rare.

- **Small-Cap Stocks**

  Stocks offered by small companies, such as start-up biotechnology companies, are known as small-cap stocks. These stocks tend to have good growth prospects but may be based on unproven (non-stable) products or services. Therefore the risk associated with these stocks is quite high. Because these companies are interested in building up their business, profits are almost always re-invested and never given as a dividend.

Mutual Funds

Mutual funds were developed as an investment tool that allowed investors the ability to pool their money together and invest in a variety of assets. Professional money managers invest this money and diversify the dollars among various types of assets. This allows the investor to enjoy the ability of spreading their funds and risk among many assets that would otherwise be cost prohibitive.

To ensure that the mutual fund is invested in the proper assets that will maximize growth within a certain acceptable risk level, a manager is appointed. All mutual funds charge a fee for this management service. The size of the fee depends on the level of management involvement. Management fees are usually charged as a percentage of the value of your mutual fund. For example, you might be charged 2 percent of the value of the fund.

Although mutual funds do offer diversity for the investor, owning one mutual fund may not provide you with enough diversity to minimize your risk. Therefore, owning several mutual funds, or investing in a family of mutual funds and spreading your funds among several mutual funds within that family can be beneficial. However, by investing in too many mutual funds, the effort and expense for diversity can become prohibitive.

As with stock, the fees and expenses associated with purchasing and selling a mutual fund tends to make investing in a mutual fund a long-term investment decision. In addition to the fees and expenses, a longer time frame is needed in order to achieve the intended results because of the diversity of mutual funds.

Listed below are brief descriptions of the various forms of funds:

- **Money Market Funds**
  Money market funds are invested primarily in short-term and high quality bonds, treasury bills, and CDs. They usually offer returns higher than a savings account but lower than a CD. The advantage of a money market accounts is the ability to withdraw money without a penalty.

- **Bond Funds**
  As discussed earlier in this section, there are a variety of bonds available for purchase. Because of this variety, there are a number of options for mutual funds based on bonds. For example, you can have a corporate bond fund, municipal bond fund, or U.S. government fund.

- **Stock Funds**
  There are a number of choices of mutual funds that invest in stocks.
  1. *Aggressive growth funds* usually invest in small companies and are typically one of the highest risk type of mutual funds. These companies almost always focus on growth and do not pay dividends.
  2. *Growth funds* usually invest in well-established companies that emphasize growth with a smaller focus on dividends.
  3. *Growth & Income funds* usually invest in firms that have some growth, but mostly focus on firms that consistently pay dividends.
  4. *Income (equity) funds* usually invest in companies that pay dividends.
  5. *Global funds* usually invest in stocks of oversea companies as well as the United States.
  6. *International funds* usually invest in strictly stocks of oversea companies.

Set-up and management fees are commonly referred to as load and no-load funds. Below is a brief description on how these fees are charged.

- **Load Fund**
  A load fund will charge either an up-front fee when the fund is purchased or redemption fee when the fund is liquidated. For instance, if you have $1,000 to invest in a fund and the fund charges an up-front fee of 3% of your initial investment, $30 will be deducted from the $1,000 and the remaining $970 will be invested.

- **No-Load Fund**
  A no-load fund will not charge up-front or redemption fees. However, many of these funds tend to charge for a variety of other services. Therefore, be sure all possible fees are explained to you before agreeing to a no-load fund.

4. ADDITIONAL RESOURCES

Listed below are additional resources that should be used when making investment decisions.

- Financial guides, such as books and magazines.
- Internet resources, such as:
  1. Company information (annual reports and press releases).
  2. Up-to-the-minute updates on stocks, bonds and mutual fund prices.
  3. Rankings of mutual funds in various categories over various time periods (one year, three-year, five-year, and ten-year).
  4. Mutual fund family information (Mutual fund companies that have their own web sites for all of the mutual funds that they sell).
- Mutual fund companies provide toll-free phone numbers so that customers can request the following information:
  1. Prospectus.
  2. Annual and/or quarterly reports.
  3. Access to customer service representatives that can answer questions.
- Financial institutions, such as banks and credit unions, provide customers a variety of information on investment choices (literature and counselors) with no charge.
- Financial advisors can be a valuable asset. They will often review your financial situation at no charge and then provide you several investment options to achieve your financial goals. This service is usually provided

at no charge because financial advisors work on commission. Therefore if you decide to purchase a mutual fund, stock, or other investment with them, they will receive a commission from the end-company that takes your order to the market. If you decide to use a financial advisor, visit with a few different advisors before making a final decision. This will provide you with more information and more choices.

5. PURCHASING INVESTMENTS

There are a number of methods to purchasing investments. Listed below are brief descriptions of some of your choices.

Full Service Broker

Full service brokers are the middle person that takes your buy and sell orders and relays them to the market. In addition, full service brokers provide you advice regarding your personal financial planning. This planning will assist you with setting goals, providing you advice on investing, and developing timelines to meet your goals. Here you should have a specific advisor who you build a relationship with.

Discount Broker

A discount broker will take your buy and sell orders to the market; however, they do not provide any form of advice or financial planning services. Discount broker services can be utilized either in person, via telephone touch phone, telephone with a live person, or via the Internet.

Internet

The Internet provides potential investors with a magnitude of choices and information regarding investing. In addition, the Internet offers many investment services at significant discounts. However, be certain you are dealing with a legitimate company before transferring personal funds to their location.

Mutual Fund Company

Most mutual fund companies allow customers to purchase a mutual fund directly, thus bypassing the full-service and discount brokers. This method can provide some cost savings depending on the type of mutual fund you purchase.

MOVING

Moving can be very stressful and expensive. This section explains how to move your belongings easily and inexpensively. In addition to the information provided about the move itself, this section also includes suggestions that will assist you in the process of establishing your new residence, such as closing and setting-up various accounts.

1. SETTING THE MOVE DATE

Setting your moving date as early as possible is the easiest thing you can do to reduce a lot of stress and headaches, as well as save yourself a lot of money. Organizing a move at the last minute can be very difficult and expensive. For example, by waiting too long to set a moving date, you may find that there are not any rental trucks available, or pay dearly for the last available truck.

2. RENTING A MOVING TRUCK

The cost of the rental truck is usually one of the largest expenses in moving, and therefore there are many opportunities to save yourself money in your move. In order to save money, you need to know the steps to take to get the best price.

Reserving your moving truck early is very important, especially if you will be moving during a popular season (spring/summer). By reserving your truck 3 to 4 months early, you will save a significant amount of money. If you are concerned that your moving date may change by a few days, inquire about the truck rental company's policy about changing reservation dates.

Collecting Rental Truck Quotes

After you have determined your moving date, follow these suggestions to obtain the most inexpensive rate on a rental truck: (A checklist is available on the next page).

- Call a reputable moving truck rental company (national chain for long distance moves).
- Inform the company of the dates you plan to move, where you are moving to, and how big of a truck you need. The company will ask you for your name, address, and telephone number. Feel free to offer this information, but do not give them any kind of credit card number or allow them to reserve your quote.
- Once the company provides you a quote, be sure to write down everything that is included in that quote, such as the rental truck price, the hand truck price, and the price for furniture pads. Also, make notes regarding the number of days and the mileage that is included with your rental.
- Next, ask about renting the truck on different days. Most often, renting a truck during the early part of the week will provide you significant savings as compared to renting on the weekend.
- Ask if the company offers discount programs, for example, belonging to an automobile association.
- Thank the company for their time and state you will consider their offer. The company will most likely try to pressure you into giving your credit card number by saying that the prices they quoted are only good if you reserve it with your credit card and that price may not be offered at a later date. Continue to thank the company and inform them that you will call back shortly.
- Call other moving truck rental companies and follow the steps above. When visiting with other companies inform them that you have visited with other companies (provide names) and state that you are looking for the best price. They most likely will be able to beat the price. However, if the savings are not significant (at least 10-15%), inform the company that the price they are offering is not sufficient for you to choose them. They will either offer to lower the price or they will not. If they can not lower the price, ask them if they can offer you better terms, such as more days on the rental or additional mileage.

MOVING QUOTE CHECKLIST

Truck Rental Company: _____

Representative's Name: _____

Date Quote Was Given: _____

Moving From: _____ **To:** _____

	Primary Move Date	Alternative Move Date	Alternative Move Date
Moving Date			
Size of Moving Truck			
Other Rentals			
Car Dolly			
Hand Truck			
Furniture Pads			
Other			
Other			
Mileage Allowed			
Cost for Additional Miles			
Number of Days Allowed			
Cost for Additional Days			
Discounts			
Coupons			
Insurance Comp. Discount			
Other			
Tax			
TOTALS			

At this point in your search all you need to do is wait. Wait for at least 24 hours before proceeding, or, if you would like, you can call more competitors and follow the same steps as listed above. The reason for waiting 24 hours is that all national truck rental franchises are connected through the computer to their national headquarters. When you provide the individual dealer with your personal information, it is sent straight to the national headquarters. Once they receive your information, your account is flagged as a non-reserved account and then you are placed on a callback list.

Being on the callback list is very advantageous because the representative from that company who calls you back has the ability to lower the price of the quote or offer other premiums in order to secure you as a customer. The rental truck company calling will generally call you within 24 hours. Many times if you are not home when they call, they will not leave a message, so you must be home, or at the number you provided them in order for the call-back process to work properly.

If you are available when one of the moving truck rental companies calls, do the following:
- Inform them that you have decided to go with another company because you were offered a lower price (be sure to mention the company by name). Also mention, that you would prefer to do business with them (the company you are speaking with), but you are on a budget and every dollar counts.
- This statement will lead them to ask what you were offered. You can do one of two things at this point:
  1. You can inform the company of your lowest quote and you will most likely get a lower price.
  2. You can inform the company that you really do not like to play the "price bidding" game, but if they were willing to drop their price by $(you fill in the number) you will make a reservation with them on the spot.

If after 24 hours has passed and you have not been called, contact the first company you received a quote from and repeat the process of quoting them your lowest quote and asking them if they can beat it.

Making A Rental Truck Reservation
When making a reservation, make sure to get the following information: (A checklist of these items is available on the next page.)
- The name of the person with whom you made the reservation.
- The date on which the reservation was made.
- A detailed quote and confirmation number.
- The company's policy for cancellations and changing rental dates.

RESERVATION INFORMATION

IMPORTANT: Request that a detailed quote be mailed to you!

Date that Reservation was made:	
Reservation Date:	
Name of Company Representative:	
Confirmation / Reservation Number:	
Cancellation Policy:	
Changing Date Policy:	

Before Picking Up Your Rental Truck
Before picking up your rental truck, remember the following:
- Call one week, as well as the day before, your reservation date to ensure that there are no problems with your reservation.
- Contact your automobile and renters' insurance provider to determine if you are in need of additional insurance coverage.

Picking Up Your Rental Truck
The day you pick up your rental truck, remember these suggestions:
- Bring your quote and reservation information along with you in case there is a discrepancy with the rental price or terms of the rental.
- Inform the rental truck company if you are in need of insurance.
- Review the interior and exterior of the truck for damages. If there are significant damages, be sure to receive documentation from the rental truck company stating that those damages occurred prior to your rental.
- Be aware of the fuel policy upon return. If the truck rental company demands that the truck be returned with a full-tank of fuel, be sure you have a full-tank of fuel before leaving with the rental truck. If they only

require that you return the truck with the same amount of fuel that was in the truck when you picked up the rental truck, then make a note of your fuel use during your move so as to not return the rental truck with a large surplus of fuel.

Moving materials
Moving materials can add up to a significant expense when moving. Below are a few suggestions to reduce that expense:

- Contact local and national chain moving companies in your area and ask if they have any used moving boxes. Sometimes they will offer them to you for free or they will sell them for a reduced price. Often these boxes are undamaged, but they may have writing on them. However, if you can save $2 to $4 per box, it may be worth the investment to just buy a colored marker (a different color than used on the box already) and re-use the box.

- Contact your local grocer and liquor store and ask when they have boxes available. Most of these locations now have compactors to crush the boxes once they are emptied, but if you call and inform them that you will stop by to pick up a few boxes, they will set them aside until you come. (Be sure to request bottled water, liquor, and produce boxes. These are very durable and often have hand holes pre-cut in them for easier handling.)

- Contact local department and electronics stores. These locations are great for providing used bubble wrap and styrofoam packaging materials.

- Search local discount stores and thrift shops for used blankets or padding materials to wrap around items that are too large to package, such as mirrors or furniture.

- Purchase tape and other packing materials you can not find at the locations listed above from hardware stores, warehouse clubs, or discount department stores. These locations will sell those materials for far less than a moving company will.

- Since most rental trucks do not come equipped with a lock for the loading door of the truck, be sure to purchase a lock. Locks can be purchased fairly inexpensively from a hardware store, warehouse club, or discount department store.

Hiring Help
Asking friends or family to help you load your truck when you move is fairly common, and by far the most inexpensive way to do it. However, what if you do not know anyone that can help you load your stuff or you do not know anyone at the location to which you are moving to help you unload? There are many places that offer assistance to load and unload your moving truck. Hiring Help

- Contact the company you are renting your moving truck from and ask if they offer these services. If they do not, ask them to refer you to a company that can assist you.
- Check for companies that offer services for "odd jobs" in the local newspaper.
- Search the Internet for moving companies in the area you are moving to. When you find a company, you can either e-mail them or call them.
- Contact your employer, school, church, or other organization for information or assistance. You never know who has a friend or family member in need of making a few extra dollars.
- Call major moving companies. Often they have a staff on hand to load and unload their own trucks. However, they sometimes contract those workers out on an hourly or half-day basis during slower periods.

3. DEDUCTING YOUR MOVING EXPENSES
One of the few advantages to moving is that under certain circumstances, you may be able to deduct many of the expenses you incur from your taxes if you meet the qualifications for the deduction. In any case, you should keep track of all your expenses and keep all of your receipts. This includes the $5 receipt for tape from the hardware store, the $50 receipt for the hotel expense, and the $16 receipt for gas. All these expenses may be allowed as deductions if you qualify. To find out if you qualify, contact the Internal Revenue Service, a local tax service or an accounting firm for more information.

4. CLOSING & SETTING-UP ACCOUNTS & SERVICES
By closing and setting-up accounts and services prior to your move, you can save yourself from a lot of headaches, late fees, and stress. This should be done no later than two weeks prior to your move. On the next page is a list of the basic accounts and services to consider closing/setting-up prior to your move.

Mail
Forwarding your mail will assist in the timely delivery of essential mail, particularly bills that will charge late fees if not paid on time.   In order to have your mail forwarded, go to your local post office and fill out a moving/forward mail form.   The form usually comes with a packet of helpful information as well as various coupons.   Also, when you arrive at your new location, the local post office may send you a packet of information including local coupons to help you settle into your new home.

Utilities (Power/Gas/Water)
Your current power, gas, and water companies will need to be informed of your move so that you are not billed for utilities used after you move. Also, you must provide a forwarding address so that the last bill, or refund, will be sent to the correct location.

As for hooking up new services, you might be able to save money on deposits by providing the new company with a letter of credit.   In most cases, deposits can add up to several hundred dollars. Almost all power/gas companies require prior services be established with them or else a deposit will be required in order to establish service.   Contact your current utility provider and request this letter of credit. Many times, if you have had service with another power/gas company for over 12 months, and your credit is good (no late bills, etc.), the deposit fee will be waived.

If you are unable to waive the deposit, be sure to mark on your calendar the date the service was started as well as the 12-month anniversary of your service. Most utility companies will return your deposit after 12 months if you have had good credit with them. However, this service is only provided upon request.

Cable Television
It is important to inform your cable television provider of your move as most cable television companies charge you prior to the month you receive the service. Therefore, by canceling your service and providing them with your new address, you will receive a timely refund check.

To avoid waiting for a refund, contact your cable television provider well before your move date (at least one month) and ask them for alternatives that you can use in order to cancel your service and by-pass the whole refund process.

Telephone - Local & Long-Distance Providers
Canceling your local telephone service is necessary to inform the company where to send your last bill. However, the long-distance telephone provider is a different scenario.

Most often, long-distance telephone providers will offer incentives for you to select them as your provider at your new location. In order to achieve the best deal in this scenario, inform yourself of the current incentives for setting up new services with long-distance telephone providers. (Refer to the "Telecommunications" section on page 106) Once you have this information, call your long-distance provider and start the negotiation process.

Financial Services (Banks/Credit Card/Loan Companies)
On some occasions your financial service providers will allow you to change your address by telephone. However, many financial services (banks/credit-cards) will only allow changes to your account in writing. This means you either have to go to the physical location and fill out forms, or you will need to send them a letter notifying them of the change. Many times, simply writing a short letter is the simplest method to make these changes. However, if you are closing your bank account, you may want to do that in person in order to receive any funds remaining in your account. Otherwise you will need to send them a letter requesting that a check for your remaining funds be mailed to you. This process can delay access to your money for several weeks.

A sample of a "change of address" letter is located on page 85. Simply copy this format with your information and mail the letter. Be sure to sign the letter or the process of changing your information will be delayed.

Other Accounts/Services

Other accounts/services that need to be notified of your move include magazine subscriptions, clubs/organizations, and any other accounts/services that communicate with you through the mail. Many times these accounts/services can be contacted by telephone. However, if they require changes to be made in writing, use the "change of address" letter below. Also, you can use the mail forwarding cards provided by the post office in the moving/forwarding packet you will receive when you fill out the moving/forwarding mail packet at the post office.

Family & Friends

Informing family and friends of your new address can be time consuming and expensive. Using e-mail, the telephone, or postcards are all quick and easy ways to update family and friends.

CHANGE OF ADDRESS LETTER

Company XYZ
Attention: Customer Service (or particular division)
1234 Whatever Street
City, State - Zip Code

Date

To Whom It May Concern:

This letter is to inform you that my address will change effective **DAY, MONTH, and Year (i.e. January 1, 2006)**. My new address, as well as any additional information required by your company, is listed below.

Your immediate response to this request for change is greatly appreciated.

Sincerely,
- (Sign your Name)
- Print Your Name
- Your Identification Number (Could be your Social Security Number or other number that identifies you to the company/organization)
- Any other particular information the company/organization requires
- Current Information
- Your Current & New Address
- Your New Information

NEGOTIATING

Negotiating is something everyone does everyday. From deciding where to eat lunch with friends, to asking for a raise at work, almost everything involves negotiation. Throughout this book there are several sections that describe specific negotiation strategies that can be used during particular situations. This section, however, will provide the reader a more general overview of the negotiation process. By implementing these simple rules, anyone can become an effective negotiator.

RULE 1 - NEGOTIATION IS NOT A COMPETITION

Many people confuse negotiating as a type of competition, which it is not. Negotiation is a process in which the parties involved try to come to a mutual agreement of the terms of a transaction or process. Although negotiation can be fun, and should be, it is not meant to be a process of one person beating the other. The best negotiations are when both parties are satisfied with the outcome of their agreement.

RULE 2 - BE PREPARED

Being prepared is the most essential element of negotiation. Preparation includes information. The amount and the type of preparation will depend entirely on what is being negotiated. For example, negotiating the price of a new car will involve an entirely different kind of preparation versus asking for a discount on piece of clothing you are interested in purchasing. Below are a few questions to consider when preparing for a negotiation.

- Who is the final decision-maker for the other party?
- What does the other party want from me?
- What do I want from the other party?
- What does the other party think I want?

- How much am I willing to pay?
- How low of a price do I think they are willing to accept?
- What are my options? (i.e. can you walk away, what are the pros and cons)
- What are the other party's options?
- What are other factors that I can negotiate on besides price?

RULE 3 - BUILD TRUST

If the person with whom you are negotiating believes you are trying to take something from them, you are not effectively negotiating. By building trust, the other person will be more open to ideas, opportunities, and suggestions that you offer.

Trust can be built several ways, but the simplest, is by appearing friendly and open, such as smiling, shaking hands, using the other persons name frequently, not crossing your arms in front of your chest (open posture), and slowly providing the other person information.

RULE 4 - DO NOT GIVE AWAY ANYTHING FOR FREE

Proper negotiation involves information. The more information, the better. So when negotiating, do not provide the other person more information than you have to. Therefore, use the give-take strategy. This strategy involves the following; if the person with whom you are negotiating asks for information, slowly provide it to them. However, ask for information in return. For example, a common question asked by salespeople is where you work and what your position is. This is an excellent question to use in determining the range of a person's income. Because this is such a personal question, and provides a lot of information about you, be sure to ask for similar valued information in return.

RULE 5 - ASK "THE" QUESTION

The easiest negotiation strategy, but one people find the hardest to do, is simply asking for what they want. If you know what you want, ask for it!

For example, when purchasing a new pair of shoes, ask the manager if you can have a free pair of socks with the purchase. The reason many people find asking such a simple question so difficult is that they are uncomfortable about what people will think. This brings us to the next rule.

RULE 6 - BE COMFORTABLE WITH NEGOTIATING

Negotiation is something our society believes is old fashioned, wrong, or cheap. We assume that the price printed on a tag or listed on a board has legitimacy and should be accepted "as is." But why? Who determined that the price on a tag or board is the price I "must" accept? But more interesting is why is a price printed on a tag or restaurant board accepted as legitimate, but the price printed on a new car window is not? This idea of one price offered to us as being legitimate, and another as not legitimate, is ridiculous. Therefore, asking for a discount, an additional free item, or added options at no additional charge should not be an uncomfortable situation.

RULE 7 - YOU HAVE POWER

Along with being comfortable with negotiating, you should understand your power. Your power is that you have something the other person wants, such as a good, service, or money. Therefore, when negotiating, always remember that you have something the other person wants. Also, if at any time, you are not satisfied with how the outcome of a negotiation is developing, state your dissatisfaction with the other party (professionally) and be prepared to walk away.

RULE 8 - BE REASONABLE

Being reasonable means to negotiate within an area that both parties believe to be acceptable. For example, if you were interested in purchasing a diamond ring that has a suggested price of $1,000, it would be unreasonable to think the jewelry dealer would accept your offer to purchase the ring for $100. However, if you suggested that you will purchase the ring for $825, the jeweler may believe that offer to be acceptable, yet may counter offer with a slightly higher price.

Sometimes what you may believe to be reasonable may not be reasonable to the other person. In this situation, you should be prepared to justify your reasoning in order to win over the other party. For example, in the diamond ring case above, you may have specific information that the particular ring you are interested in can be purchased by jewelers from a supplier for $800 to $850. Therefore, if the jeweler is offended, or laughs at your offer of $825, justify your reasoning by stating to the jeweler that you are aware of the wholesale pricing for that particular ring ($800) and believe you should be able to purchase it for slightly more than that amount.

RULE 9 - SILENCE IS YOUR FRIEND

Many people hate silence because it makes them uncomfortable. However, silence is a key strategy in negotiating and the better you handle it, the better you will become at negotiating. This is a common strategy by professional sales people to get the other party to provide them additional information.

Consider this. When you make an offer or counteroffer, the other person may just look at you in silence. Professional sales people and negotiators understand people are uncomfortable in this situation and will do this simply to get the other party to provide them additional information. When this occurs, do not assume they are waiting for more information from you. If the person truly wanted more information from you, they would ask you for it. Therefore, simply wait and let them make the next move.

RULE 10 - DO NOT LEAVE ANYTHING ON THE TABLE

If you are willing to purchase a certain item for $10 and your offer is accepted easily, be hesitant in agreeing to the deal. The reason is that the other person may have more to offer you than you are aware of. Therefore, ask more questions. Remember that information is the key to negotiating.

PURCHASING A CAR

A car can be one of the more expensive items that you will purchase during your lifetime. Therefore, it is worth the time and effort to ensure you are making the best decision possible when deciding upon the type of car to buy as well as from whom you should buy the car. By following the suggestions on the following pages, your car buying experience should be much more enjoyable and affordable.

1. CREATE A BUDGET

The first step in purchasing a car is determining the type of car you can afford. Creating a budget is the best way to accomplish this task. Be sure to refer to the "Budgeting" section on page 11 to determine the type of car you can afford. Be careful though, the monthly payment of your new car is not the only expense associated with your purchase. Below are a few of the other expenses associated with a new car that you should consider.

- Down Payment
- Finance Costs
- Gasoline
- Insurance

- Licensing Fees
- Registration Fees
- Repairs & Maintenance
- Taxes

You should be able to find estimates for these expenses either by searching the Internet, visiting you local car dealer and insurance agent, and visiting your state Department of Transportation and Department of Taxation.

2. CHOOSING THE RIGHT CAR

The following are questions to consider when deciding on what type of car is right for you.

- How many miles will be driven annually?
- How often will the car be used on a daily basis?
- Will the car be used primarily on the highway or in the city?
- How many passengers will travel with you on a regular basis?
- How important is safety?
- Is reliability essential?

Your answers to these questions should help narrow your search considerably. In addition, by also adding your budget to these answers, you will be provided with enough information to determine the model and age of car(s) you should be considering.

3. NEW VERSUS USED CARS

The choice of a new versus a used car will depend a lot on your priorities and budget. For example, if reliability is a high priority, you may think a new car is the obvious choice. This is not always the case. There are many used cars on the market that are rated as extremely reliable, whereas some new cars have quite the opposite rating. Listed below are some generalities to consider when deciding between a new or used car. But be careful, these are just generalities and further research should be conducted before making a final decision.

New Cars
- Usually more expensive
- Include standard warranties

Used Cars
- Usually less expensive (*purchase price and insurance costs*)
- Warranties are mostly non-existent if you purchase the car from a private individual. However, many used car dealerships now offer limited warranties.
- Maintenance expenses will usually be higher

4. RESEARCHING A CAR

The Internet has become a valuable tool for conducting research on cars. Industry magazines are also a great resource to use, primarily for newer models. On the next page are a few areas to begin researching.

Dealer's Cost and Manufacturer's Suggested Retail Price (MSRP)
When researching for a new car, there are a number of Internet sites that allow you to determine both the dealer's cost and MSRP for a car. Also be sure to familiarize yourself with the costs of the car's options. Knowing these prices will play an important role when negotiating with a salesperson.

Book Value/Fair Market Value of Car
Because of the size and diversity of the automobile industry, a number of companies have been created to assist consumers and dealers in determining the fair market value for a new or used car. Many of these companies have websites on the Internet as well as published versions of their research (*hence the term "book value"*). In most cases, the value of a car is based on the quality of care that car has received over its life, its current mileage, and its options. Therefore, when you find the model and age of the car you are looking for, you will most likely be given a low, average and high value for the car. These values are important to know, not only for negotiating a purchase or trade-in value, but also for financing. In many cases, banks and other financial institutions will only loan you an amount equal to the lowest book value.

Car Review Reports
Many Internet sites, as well as industry magazines, publish various car review reports. These companies produce reports based on a variety of tests, including driving and crash tests. In addition, they will rank items such as MSRP, dealer cost, target price, insurance costs, service costs, and future resale value.

Vehicle History Reports
Becoming more common on the Internet are companies offering vehicle history reports. For a small fee, these companies will provide you a report of previous owners, accidents, and other relevant information about a car's history. Usually the only information needed to conduct this research is the vehicle's identification number, make, model, and year it was produced.

5. VISITING THE DEALERSHIP
Visiting a dealership to further research your options is often viewed as an intimidating process, but it does not need to be. All you have to remember is that you are the one with the power. The power to say, "Yes" or "No."

Make the dealership earn your business, not force you to do business with them. Below are some tips to consider when visiting a dealership.

- Be prepared. Know the type of car you are looking for and what you want to accomplish while at the dealership (*test drive, obtain literature, check prices, etc.*).

- Be up front about your goals. For example, inform the salesperson that you are considering purchasing a car and have done some research and need the following items (*test drive, literature, etc.*). Also let them know that you are not ready to make a decision until you have evaluated all your options and gathered all your information. If they press you for what information you are gathering and from what sources, just tell them what you need from them. Do not feel like you need to share your other considerations with them unless you want to get their feedback.

- Do not be pressured into making a quick decision. Many dealers will push "one-time sales" or "special deals" to encourage you to buy now. If your not ready, simply inform the salesperson that you would rather spend more money and make the best decision versus being rushed into saving a few dollars. Remember, sales are always occurring and are often used as gimmicks to get people into the dealership.

- In order to test-drive a car, some dealers may require a signature or a copy of your driver's license. Be sure to question why they need this information and what it is used for. If you are asked to sign a document, read it very carefully. If you have any doubts about what you are signing, – do not sign! You can always go to another dealership.

- When test driving, take the car somewhere familiar to you. You want to know how the car will handle in your environment, not the dealer's.

- Visit more than one dealer in order to compare prices, selection and customer service.

6. PURCHASING A USED CAR FROM A DEALER

Although purchasing a used car from a dealer does provide some security, you must remember that a used car is a car that someone else no longer wanted. Therefore, you should make every effort to try and find out if there are any problems with the car you want to purchase. Below are some tips to help with this process.

- Look for cars with lower mileage
- Evaluate purchasing an extended warranty for added protection

- Research the number of previous owners the car has had. Multiple owners may be a signal of a problem car.
- Before finalizing a sale of a used car, be sure to have all agreements in writing, such as the sales price, payment terms and repairs to be completed.
- If you are concerned that you are not getting straight answers about the condition of the car you are interested in, follow the recommendations in the next section.

7. PURCHASING A CAR FROM A NON-DEALER

Purchasing a car from a non-dealer, such as from the classifieds, can be a risky venture; however, there are also good deals to be found. If you are considering this option, be sure to obtain a professional opinion of the car's condition before purchasing it. For example, contact a local car repair shop you trust and inform them that you are considering purchasing a car and would like them to evaluate its condition. This may cost you a little money, but it will be well worth it in the long run. Next, you will need to coordinate obtaining the car from the seller to the shop for evaluation. If the seller has a problem allowing you to have the car evaluated, inform them that they can be present at the time of the evaluation. If they continue to resist, then you are probably better off considering another car.

Once the car is evaluated, have the repairperson provide you with a list of problems as well as estimates to repair them. Use this information in your negotiation process. See the "Negotiating" section on page 86.

8. TRADING-IN VERSUS SELLING YOUR CAR

In almost every situation involving a trade-in, you will receive significantly less than you believe your trade-in to be worth. The reason for this is that the dealer must invest resources into your trade-in, such as a tune-up and a safety check, in order to resell your car. In addition, they will incur a number of expenses associated with selling your car, such as advertising and commission fees. Therefore, the dealer must subtract these costs from what it believes it can reasonably sell your trade-in for.

The alternative to using your current car as a trade-in is to sell it yourself. However, before deciding on this option, consider these items:

- Trading in a car is very quick and convenient.
- Privately selling your car could result in a better value, but could also result in you investing a lot of your time trying to sell your old car.
- It is very difficult to coordinate the timing of the sale of your old car and the purchase of your new car. If there is a delay you could not have the money for a down payment or be without a car for a period of time.
- Trading in your car will result in tax savings if the state that you live in has sales tax. For instance, if you purchase a car for $20,000 and trade in a car worth $5,000, sales tax will only be based on the $15,000 difference.

9. PURCHASING VS. LEASING A CAR

The debate between purchasing a car outright versus leasing a car really comes down to your personal preference. There are numerous advantages and disadvantages to both. This section is written to help you determine which option is best for you.

Purchase Option

Unless you have a stockpile of cash that has no better use to you, then you may want to use it to purchase your car outright. For the rest of us, we will need to find someone to lend us the money. Banks and credit unions are the most common locations to find loans for new and used cars, but almost all dealers offer financing programs as well. In most cases, bank and credit union loan options are much more competitive and flexible than a dealer. However, because of the competitiveness in the auto financing market, it is in your best interest to compare all your loan options before making a decision.

To determine if purchasing your new car is the best option consider these advantages and disadvantages.

Buying Advantages:
- No mileage penalty
- You can sell your car whenever you wish
- Purchasing a car is usually more economical if you intend to keep it for a long period of time

Buying Disadvantages:
- A high down payment may be required
- Higher monthly payments are required
- A larger portion of you money is tied-up in a car, rather than in investments which usually appreciate, costing you money

Lease Option
Leasing cars has become increasingly popular among consumers because of the advantages described below. Yet even with its popularity, it is not an option for everyone. Leases among dealers are not consistent and can be confusing. When considering a lease, be sure to have the requirements and fees of the lease explained to you. For example, have the dealer write out the expected total to be paid for the term of the lease so you can better understand you financial expectations. In addition, be sure to consider all of the advantages and disadvantages of a lease as described below:

Lease Advantages:
- Lower monthly payments
- Less maintenance problems
- Lower down payment
- An easy method to establish credit
- Once you lease, you never have to sell your old car
- You can get into a new car every two to three years

Lease Disadvantages:
- The cost of leasing in the long-term is usually more expensive than the cost of purchasing an car
- Finance charges are usually confusing
- Mileage limits exist
- You might not be eligible for rebates
- The selling price is usually the MSRP
- Insurance premiums are usually higher
- Excess wear and tear fees exist
- Program maintenance responsibilities
- Even after making payments for the term of the lease you do not own the car
- If your driving habits change, it is difficult to change/terminate a lease

10. NEGOTIATING

As mentioned in the "Negotiating" section on page 86, research is the key to a successful negotiation. This is especially true when negotiating for a new car. Once complete, your research will provide you a fair price you can expect to pay for your new car, the value of your trade-in and the type of finance options available. Put this information together and create a negotiation package you believe to be fair and within your budget. The next step is taking your negotiation package to the dealer.

When negotiating with the dealer, be aware that they often work on incentives (*commissions*) on different areas of the sale. These areas include:
1. Negotiating the price of the new car
2. Negotiating the price of the trade-in car (*See item 8 on page 94*)
3. Financing (*see item 9 on page 95*)

So what might seem like a great deal on the price of the new car, may be made up on a not-so-great deal on your trade-in or financing. Therefore, remember that negotiating the purchase of a car is a multi-step process. To try and confuse you during your negotiation, some dealers will try and bundle all the steps together. Avoid this if at all possible and negotiate each step separately. The steps should be negotiated in the order listed above.

11. OTHER CONSIDERATIONS

First Time Car Buyer & Recent College Graduate Discounts
Many car manufacturers offer discounts on new car purchases to first time car buyers and recent college graduates. During your research process, be sure to inquire about these discounts and add them to the negotiation package you created. If you discover a rebate program soon after you have purchased your vehicle, be sure to request that the rebate be honored.

Customer Service
Even though obtaining the best price on a car is important, equally important is the service that comes with your car. There is nothing worse than having a problem with your car and having it take several days/weeks to resolve, if ever. Therefore, be sure to research the customer satisfaction of dealers you are considering purchasing from. For example, do they offer replacement cars while yours is in the shop or do they offer pick-up and delivery service when your car is in need of repair.

RECORD RETENTION

Retaining important and pertinent family and business documents saves time, money, and frustration. Many of these documents have financial value, as well as personal value. Therefore, ensuring that they are safe is very important.

Documents such as those listed below should be kept in a secure location, such as a fireproof safe or a bank safe-deposit box. If you have questions regarding the specific time frame documents should be kept, ask the organization affiliated with that document for their recommendation.

- Social security cards
- Passports and citizen papers
- Divorce decrees
- Stock and bond certificates
- Automobile titles
- Titles and deeds
- Appraisals
- Bank Statements
- Birth certificates
- Marriage licenses
- Military papers
- Copies of past tax returns
- Insurance policies
- Lease documents
- Photography negatives
- Credit Card Statements
- Inventory listing of items in your home for insurance purposes

RENTAL CARS

When you reserve a rental car, the prices that you are initially quoted are usually inflated considerably. The suggestions provided below will assist you in receiving the lowest possible rate. Remember that the initial quoted price is only the starting point for determining the price that you will pay.

1. BOOKING YOUR RENTAL CAR

Below are methods to use to locate the lowest rates on car rentals.

- Book your rental car in advance to avoid a high price due to a low availability of vehicles.
- Check rental rates for major car-rental companies on the Internet. Most web-sites will advertise special promotional rates.
- Attempt to rent your car either over a five day, week, or weekend period to avoid paying high one-day rental rates.
- Shop around for the best deals by contacting all of the rental-car companies.
- When traveling to a location frequently or for a long period of time, contact regional rental-car companies or local car dealers, as they may be able to offer a better value for rental cars.
- Inquire about rates at various locations within the same city. For instance, request prices for picking up the rental car at a downtown location, the airport, or suburban locations.

2. DISCOUNTS

Listed below are various discounts you may be eligible for when renting a car.

- Join as many frequent-renter programs as possible to receive discounts off the rental price, free upgrades, faster check-in, and frequent-flier miles.

- Mention associations and corporations that you belong to for possible discounts.
- Inquire about discounts affiliated with a frequent-flier program.
- Inquire about special promotional rates, such as off-season rates.
- Locate coupons in frequent-flier program newsletters or association newsletters.

3. CAR RENTAL INSURANCE

Before renting a car, contact your personal automobile insurance company to inquire about car rental insurance coverage. In many cases you will not need to purchase additional insurance from the rental car company. In addition, contact your renter's insurance agent about theft or vandalism coverage. Finally, contact your credit card company prior to the car rental to determine if your card covers car-rental insurance. Many gold cards do cover car rental insurance; however, some credit card rental insurance applies only to certain car-rental agencies.

4. "DRIVE AWAY" CARS

During the "off peak" seasons, many rental car companies have an overabundance of vehicles in the wrong areas of the country. Therefore, in order to get these cars to the correct areas, these companies will provide significant incentives to people who are willing to drive these cars to another part of the country where they are needed. For example, a rental car company location in Maine may have too many cars in stock during the early winter and have a tremendous need for them in Florida. In order to get those cars to Florida, the company has two choices. One is to hire a truck to haul the cars to Florida. Or the company can have someone rent the car and drive it "one-way" to Florida.

Obviously, the second choice is more beneficial to the company because it provides the company some income. However, it is difficult to locate customers willing to drive a car "one-way" because the customer, if intending to return to the original point of departure, will need to find another means of transportation back. However, if you have a flexible schedule and if the return transportation and the incentive to take a "drive away" car to another location is reasonable, this may be a viable option for you.

5. PICKING UP YOUR RENTAL CAR

When picking up your rental car there are a number of factors to keep in mind before leaving with your rental car.

- Be aware of the car's return policy, for example, if you are required to return the vehicle with a full tank of fuel and by what time the vehicle must be returned on the return date.
- Check the vehicle's fuel gauge. Be sure it designates that there is a full tank of fuel, particularly if you are responsible for returning the car with a full tank of fuel.
- If being charged for mileage, note that the mileage odometer is correct with the odometer reading on your rental contract.
- Be sure to look at the vehicle thoroughly for damages. If there are damages, have the customer service agent note them on your rental contract as well as sign and print their name to ensure that you are protected from being charged for these damages.
- If you are unhappy with the vehicle provided for any reason, ask for a different vehicle. If they do not have a comparably priced vehicle available, request to be given a larger (upgraded) vehicle at no additional charge. If they are not willing to assist you, ask to speak with a supervisor or to be connected by telephone to their national headquarters.

6. RETURNING YOUR RENTAL CAR

To ensure that you will not be charged additional fees for your rental, be sure to consider these factors.

- Inform the customer service agent of any problems you had with the vehicle and request compensation for the problem, such as a credit on your bill or a coupon for a free rental. In some instances, the customer service agent may not be able to assist you. If not, ask to speak to a supervisor. Be sure to have your rental vehicle identification information, the location from where you rented and returned the vehicle, and the name of the customer service agent you spoke to about the problem.
- Most car rental companies require the vehicle to be returned with a full tank of fuel. If you do not return the vehicle with a full tank of fuel, your rental contract may state that they can charge you an additional amount for filling the fuel tank. The charge for this can be three to four times the fair market price of fuel.

- When returning your rental vehicle after business hours, be sure to provide them with the keys using a piece of paper or envelope that states the time you returned the vehicle.

7. OTHER CONSIDERATIONS

- Request vehicles with low mileage, to reduce the risk of car problems.
- When making a reservation, be sure to ask for the amount of additional fees such as taxes and airport concession fees, since those amounts may not be included in the initial quote.
- Inquire about extra charges such as an "additional driver" charge.
- Compact cars may not be worth the minimal savings, especially if they result in only a $3 to $5 difference in price per day. Therefore, you might want to consider a larger-size car for safety and / or comfort.
- Wednesdays tend to be the most expensive one-day rental day during the week because of business travelers.

RENTER'S INSURANCE

When you are renting an apartment, condominium, townhouse, or house, your landlord's insurance policy, in most cases, will only insure the building, not any of your personal belongings. Therefore, as a tenant you must determine if you feel comfortable repaying for all your belongings should a fire or other disasters destroy your possessions. In addition, you might also have to defend yourself against a liability lawsuit. For instance, someone may slip on some water on the floor in your apartment, require expensive medical services, and decide to sue you. Considering that the average renter's insurance policy costs between $150 and $250 per year, renter's insurance is a very inexpensive safeguard.

1. DETERMINING THE VALUE OF YOUR BELONGINGS
When you contact an insurance company for quotes on renter's insurance, one of the first questions they will ask you will be the amount of insurance you will require. Therefore, prior to contacting an insurance company, complete the chart on the next page to determine an estimated value of your personal belongings.

2. "ACTUAL" VERSUS "COST-VALUE"
Once you have completed the chart regarding the value of your belongings, you should consider the type of renter's insurance you want. There will be a significant difference in the price of the two options; however, you must consider what the two options are providing before you make your choice.

Actual-Cash-Value
Actual-cash-value policies reimburse you only for the value of the property when it was destroyed or stolen.

Replacement-Cost-Value

Replacement-cost-value polices will reimburse you the actual amount to replace your damaged or stolen property. Some policies also allow the insurance company the option to replace your damaged or stolen property with replacement property, equal to or greater than the value of the damaged or stolen property.

Detailed Inventory of Your Personal Belongings

Category	Example of Items	Purchase Price	Replacement Price
Electronics	Computers, TVs, VCRs, Phones, Fax Machines, Printers, Stereos		
Furniture	Bedroom, Living Room, Dining Room, Kitchen		
Appliances	Microwave, Refrigerator, Dishwasher, Washer, Dryer, Blenders		
Collectibles	Stamps, Antiques, Baseball Cards		
Jewelry	Engagement Rings, Wedding Rings, Gold		
Exercise Equip	Treadmills, Weight Sets		
Other	Tools, CDs, China		

3. REDUCING YOUR RENTER'S INSURANCE

Below are suggestions to consider when searching for renter's insurance.
- Shop around for policies and compare premiums.
- Consider increasing your deductible.
- Combine your automobile and renter's insurance policies if the insurance company offers discounts for joint policies.
- Consider adding "protective devices", such as fire and smoke detectors, fire extinguishers, dead-bolt locks, and alarm systems if the insurance company offers discounts for these devices.

- Insurance companies may provide a discount if you mention that you live within a gated community.
- Installing a sophisticated home-security system may result in a 15 to 20 percent discount.
- Inquire about group coverage for associations or organizations that you belong to.
- Remain with the same insurance company for continuous years, as some companies will offer discounts to faithful customers. This does not mean that you shouldn't comparison shop. However, it does mean that after comparison shopping, you should consult your current insurance company about your findings before changing services.

4. REGISTERING YOUR BELONGINGS

Once you have obtained renter's insurance, you need to take a detailed inventory of your personal belongings. This will assist in the process of obtaining your insurance claim. The chart provided on the previous page will assist with this process.

Any additional information that describes your personal belongings will be helpful in obtaining possible insurance claims. Photographs, video recordings, owner's manuals, and receipts are all great resources of information. Once you accumulate all this information, store it in a safe location, such as a fireproof safe or a bank safe-deposit box. In addition, keeping a second copy in a separate location is a good idea.

5. OTHER CONSIDERATIONS

Consider some of the topics below when visiting with insurance companies, as these can affect the price and type of insurance coverage you select.

- Insurance companies will inquire if you have pets. The answer to this question is used to determine if your pet is a risk to attacking someone. This can increase your insurance significantly.
- Inform your insurance company of any expensive personal items, such as jewelry, antiques, and electronics. Insurance companies usually place limits on the recover of single items (usually $1,000). As a result, you should inquire about purchasing a separate "insurance rider" or "personal article floater" for expensive items that might not be covered under your normal renter's insurance.

TELECOMMUNICATIONS

Telecommunication encompasses a broad range of communication devices and services. This section will focus primarily on local and long distance telephone companies, telephone calling cards, cellular telephones, and Internet access services. Below are suggestions and techniques to save money and/or reduce your expenses when using these services.

1. LOCAL TELEPHONE SERVICE

Generally, local telephone companies offer the same services from region to region. However, there are still many opportunities to save a significant amount of money. Below are a few methods to consider when establishing new local telephone service, or evaluating your current service.

Calling Plans

Understand the calling plan options, if any, the telephone company offers. For example, some companies may offer a plan that entitles you to unlimited calls for a flat monthly fee, whereas another plan may offer you a limited number of local calls a month for half the price of the unlimited call plan. Also inquire about trial periods for the calling plans. Some companies allow customers to change their calling plan once, or within a certain time frame, without incurring a fee. If you are offered a trial period, be sure to note when that trial period concludes and evaluate the calling plan prior to that date.

Service Plans

Most local telephone companies offer the option to purchase a "service insurance plan". This plan usually covers any repair expenses that may be needed within your home should it be needed, such as damaged telephone wires or telephone jacks. Although this service is usually offered for a minimal fee, you must determine if the service is needed.   Consider the following suggestions before agreeing to purchase the service plan:

- Many property management groups offer telephone service as part of your monthly rent. Therefore, contact your property manager to see if this service is available to you.

- Ask the local telephone company the expense if a service call were needed. Evaluate the expense of that potential call versus not paying the monthly fee. Sometimes the potential expense of a service call is worth the savings of not paying a monthly fee.

Calling Options

As technology increases, the options available from your local telephone company increase as well.   Three-way calling, call waiting, caller-ID, unlisted telephone numbers, and voicemail are just a few of options available to telephone service subscribers. Before agreeing to purchase an option, consider some of the following suggestions.

- When evaluating the service on the basis of a monthly payment, the expense appears minimal.   Instead, calculate out the expense of the option over the period of one year.   If the option still appears reasonable, and you believe that you will use the option, then consider purchasing it.

- Some telephone companies will offer packages that include two popular options along with an additional option that is not so popular for slightly more than the price if you had just purchased the two options alone. Although this may sound like a deal, consider how much you would truly use that third, less desirable, option. If you believe you will rarely use the third option, only purchase the two options you want.

- Consider what options, if any, you want prior to contacting the telephone company. Often telephone service providers will offer you the ability to try a calling option for a period of time, with the ability to cancel the service without penalty.   However, this offer may only be available when establishing new telephone service.

Picking A Long Distance Telephone Carrier

When establishing new service with a local telephone company, they will usually ask you to inform them of the long distance telephone carrier you prefer. Inform the local telephone company that you will contact a long distance telephone company directly to have service established, then refer to the next section.

2. LONG DISTANCE TELEPHONE SERVICE

Unlike local telephone companies, long distance telephone companies no longer enjoy the benefits of limited competition. Therefore, long distance companies compete for customers. Ever since the de-regulation of long distance telephone services, companies have continually reduced their prices, changed calling plans, and offered better technology in order to obtain new customers, or retain current customers. Because of this competition for customers, long distance users have a certain amount of bargaining power. This section describes suggestions on how to use your bargaining power to achieve significant savings on your long distance telephone use.

Evaluate Your Long Distance Telephone Use
Determine when you make your calls. Are they made during the weeknights, weekends, throughout the day, or scattered throughout the week? Determining this will provide you valuable information as to the calling plan that will best meet your needs and provide you the best savings.

Consider Changing Your Long Distance Calling Pattern
For example, there are many plans that offer considerable discounts for calls made during the weekends. If you do not mind waiting until the weekend to make the majority of your long distance telephone calls, then these types of plans may save you a significant amount of money. Also, you can consider using a 10-10-number during the week, as described in the "10-10 numbers" section on page 111, to reduce the expense of your weekday calls.

Re-Evaluate Your Calling Plan
Spending a few minutes on the telephone every few months negotiating with long distance companies is a small price to pay for significant savings. To properly prepare for this negotiation process, you need to be informed of what offers are currently available. Listed below are suggestions for preparation.

- Collect offers you receive in the mail. Some companies will mail you checks (once deposited you agree to automatically switch long distance telephone service) or offers to receive gifts if you switch long distance services.

- Search the Internet. All of the major long distance companies have web-sites that describe their offers, as well as additional offers if you sign up for their service through their web-site. Offers through web-sites will usually include a significant discount, but in exchange for certain options. For example, your monthly billing may only be sent to you by e-mail and/or you may have to agree to have your monthly bill paid by credit card.

- Ask other people. Because there are so many offers available for long distance telephone service, you may not be able to know about them all. Therefore, ask your friends and family about offers they are receiving.

- Do not be afraid to ask for more. Most of the representatives you speak with when discussing new service have some ability to negotiate or offer special incentives. For example, ask the representative to have any monthly fees tied to a specific calling plan waived or provide you with some frequent-flier mileage. If they are hesitant or say they do not have the authority, ask for someone that does (i.e. supervisor).

- Accept long distance solicitations by telephone. Although these calls can be annoying, if properly used, they can save you a lot of money and/or provide you some great gifts. Therefore, always be aware of the conditions of your current program so you can compare the offers. Again, do not be afraid to ask for more than the person is offering. Often the best question before you agree to switch service is "....well, I would switch, I just wish there was something more you could offer me".

- After you have negotiated your best deal, ask to have some time to think over the decision if you need. You can request that the representative call you back, or get the representative's name and number and you can call them back. This will provide you time to think over your decision and/or call your current long distance telephone provider to negotiate with them a similar offer so that you do not have to change your long distance service.

- After evaluating your long distance telephone service options, you may decide that your current plan/company is still the best option for you. This does not mean that you cannot negotiate with them for an even better deal. Therefore, contact your current long distance provider and inform them of specific offers you have received, such as a $75 check from a competitor if you change your long distance service to their company. State that you are contemplating switching your service to that company unless they are willing to provide you with a similar incentive to stay. If they are hesitant in offering you anything, provide them suggestions, such as a specific amount of credit placed on your account, $15 credit on your monthly bill for the next four months, waiver of your monthly fee, or free gift.

• Be aware of monthly charges. Many of the long distance calling plans available are offered in conjunction with small monthly fees. If there are any monthly fees associated with the calling plan request that the fees be waived. If refused, ask if you can have the fees waived for at least a few months.

3. "SLAMMING"

"Slamming" is a term referring to the process of a long distance company automatically switching your long distance service to their company without your knowledge. This has become so common that legislation has been introduced in Congress to establish laws to control the use of this process.

To stop "Slamming", contact your local telephone company. Local telephone companies have developed a system where you inform them of the long distance telephone company you want to have provide service and that you do not want that company changed unless you call to request that change.

If you have been "Slammed", contact the long distance telephone company you had prior to the slamming and inform them of the situation. Ask the company to have your long distance plan re-instated and to provide you with details to ensure that you will not be overcharged for telephone calls that you made with the other long distance telephone company. In most cases, you will have to contact the long distance telephone company that "slammed" you to work out the details of any overcharges.

4. CALLING CARDS & PREPAID CALLING CARDS

Calling cards and prepaid calling cards are a great option to have when traveling away from home. The problem with a calling card or a prepaid calling card is determining which one is the best. Not only do the standard long distance telephone companies offer their own calling cards, but almost every other company, from warehouse clubs to gas stations, offer their own prepaid calling card. Because of this diverse variety of choices the only suggestion available is to compare the current offers available. Below are questions to consider when reviewing your options.

• What is the charge per minute?

- Are calls rounded up to a minute, half-minute, or other?
- Is there a charge for each time I use the card?

Considerations For Prepaid Calling Cards

- If you believe that minutes were deducted incorrectly, contact the toll-free phone number on the back of the card and request that the customer service representative add your minutes back onto your card.
- Many prepaid calling cards now allow customers to add minutes to their card when the minutes have expired. You can usually contact the prepaid calling card company directly and charge the dollar amount to your credit card account. This is much more convenient than purchasing a new prepaid calling card.

5. INFORMATION (OPERATOR ASSISTANCE)

Using Information to find a telephone number is a premium priced service. However, you do not have to use the standard 555-1212 number in order to find a telephone number. Listed below are methods to use when trying to locate a telephone number.

Use The Internet

Whether locating the telephone number of a person or a business, the information you need is easier and easier to find on the Internet. Simply use one of the more popular search engines and use the "white pages" or "yellow pages" option. Type in the needed information and let the search engine find the telephone number for you. Chances are that if you are unable to locate the information on the Internet, using Information will likely not locate the phone number either.

Locating A Business

When locating a business, an additional option to use besides the Internet is the 1-800 directory. Simply call 1-800-555-1212 and ask for the toll-free number for the company you desire. There is no charge for this call.

6. 10-10 NUMBERS

10-10 numbers are fairly new to the spectrum of telephone long distance choices available. 10-10 numbers are access codes used in order to make a long distance call without using your normal long distance telephone company. Using 10-10 numbers is a great option, and if used effectively, can save you a significant amount. Below are some suggestions and warnings to consider before using 10-10 numbers.

Be Sure The Person/Business Is Available
Some 10-10 numbers charge a flat fee for a certain amount of time. For example, a call for 25 minutes will cost only $1. The problem is that you will be charged this amount if you talk for a ½ minute or 25 minutes. Thus, if the person or business is not available, and you get their answering machine, you just paid $1 for a ½ minute call. Therefore, try to arrange a time to call if possible, or call using your regular long distance carrier to ensure the person/business you are trying to contact is available.

Use A Stopwatch
Since many 10-10 number offers are correlated with time limits, it is to your advantage to have a stopwatch, or other timepiece, available to warn you of the time limit. Try stopping your conversation at least 10-15 seconds prior to the end of your time limit. This will assist in making sure your call will be completed prior to the time limit and ensure you will not be charged for an additional minute.

Call-Back Versus Continuing
If you believe your conversation will continue past the designated time of the 10-10 offer, consider calling the person back again versus continuing on with the conversation. By continuing on with the conversation, you may be paying twice the amount you have paid had you just called back.

Search The Internet
There are more and more 10-10 numbers originating everyday. To make sure you are getting the best offer on a 10-10 number, search the Internet. Many of the companies that provide these 10-10 numbers advertise their products on-line and also maintain web pages.

7. CELLULAR TELEPHONES
The safety and convenience, as well as the prestige associated with cellular telephones has created a large demand for these products and services. As with local and long distance telephone companies, cellular telephone companies offer a variety of choices. Below are some tips to assist you in choosing the best cellular telephone program for your needs.

Selecting A Service Provider And Plan
Spending time researching the best service provider and plan for your needs will make your life a lot easier and will save you a lot of money. The following are some tips to consider in your research.

- **Service Area**
  There are many options for service providers, such as local, regional and national companies. Before choosing a provider, evaluate where you believe you will use your cellular telephone the most. Also, be sure to consider the service provider's expandability from its current coverage area. For example, do they have plans to grow their existing service area?

- **Competition**
  As with long distance telephone companies, cellular companies are always offering better and better deals on their programs as time goes on. This means you will need to shop around, compare prices, and negotiate. You can learn more about negotiating by reading the section on "Negotiating" on page 86.

- **Recommendations**
  Personal recommendations from reliable resources are almost always the best source of information. Visit with friends and family that currently have cellular telephones and ask them for advice and opinions. Not only can you find out some of the best deals currently available, but you may also learn about different scams or service problems people are experiencing.

- **Consider Your Budget**
  As with any purchase, be sure that a cellular program fits into your budget. To learn more about budgeting, read the "Budgeting" section on page 11. Often companies will advertise low priced programs to bring in new customers, but fail to inform them about the numerous taxes and fees that are going to be added. These taxes and fees can easily exceed 10-percent of the advertised rates that was being offered. Therefore, be sure to have the sales representative specifically describe to you your total monthly recurring expenses and the fees for any miscellaneous services you may use, such as roaming and long distance.

- **Upgrading & Downgrading Service Plans**
  The most important factor to remember with upgrading and downgrading service plans is that upgrading is much easier than downgrading. In fact, some companies will charge you a significant fee for downgrading a service plan. Therefore, if you are unsure about the amount of usage you need, start with a smaller plan and increase it as necessary. Also, avoid

being pushed into a larger plan. Most sales representatives will tell you that you have a certain period of time after your purchase to change your service plan without any penalty then convince you to start with a larger service plan. Their hope is that you will forget to change your service plan or that you will become accustomed to the larger plan and not want to change to a smaller version. Thus spending more money than you had originally anticipated.

- **Signing & Reviewing A Contract**
  Most companies now require you to commit to a service plan for a specific amount of time. If you fail to meet your requirements of the service plan, you may be subject to a significant penalty. Therefore, before signing a contract, be sure you completely understand your requirements. Also look for items that are confusing. Be sure to have someone explain these items to you until you understand it. If you are concerned, or have doubts, do not sign.

Select the Right Phone

Just like everything else in the telecommunication market, there are a lot of choices, and cellular telephones are no different. Many of the features on cellular telephones are really up to your personal preferences. However, you should understand that the smaller the telephone, the more expensive that it should be. The best method to determine what cellular telephone is best for you is to try them out. Most cellular telephone retailers have their phones on display. This is a great way to find the phone that fits your needs. In addition, there are some companies that will even allow you to "try-out" the cellular phones for an extended period of time.

8. INTERNET SERVICE

Internet service providers often have several Internet access options available to subscribers. Frequently people will purchase service plans that offer them many more options than they require and also pay quite a bit more than they need. For most people, having simple access to the Internet and an e-mail account is all they need. Below are a few suggestions to consider in order to save money on Internet and e-mail service.

National Internet Providers

National Internet providers usually charge premium prices for their services because of name recognition and the option package they provide. Many of the options they provide to users are usually found for free and can be accessed by anyone on the Internet. However, if you travel often, you may want to utilize a national Internet provider since you might save money by being able to use a toll-free phone number.

Local Internet Providers
Local Internet providers usually offer several option packages at very reasonable prices. These savings are justified by limited advertising and low overhead. However, ask for references before purchasing a service plan to ensure you are working with a reputable company.

Contracts
Avoid long-term contracts unless there is a significant discount available for doing so. Most Internet providers only offer billing periods on a month-to-month basis; however, many do offer one-year contracts for a significant savings. If you are considering a one-year contract, be sure to ask what options you have when moving, or if you need to cancel service for a period of time, such as if your computer crashes and it takes several months before you can have it fixed.

Discounts
Because of the competitive market, Internet companies are struggling to maintain customers in order to build their companies. This offers customers a significant ability to negotiate. Therefore, as mentioned in the "Long Distance Telephone Service" section on page 108, re-evaluate your Internet plan occasionally to make sure you are getting the best deal available.

Changing Your E-mail Address
The hassle of changing e-mail address is the most common reason people continue to stay with an Internet company, even though there are cheaper options available. Changing your email address is no different than moving. Sure you have to inform everyone that you changed your address, but the process simply involves sending out a broadcast message stating "my new address is XYZ@1234".

Free Email
Many Internet web-sites offer users free email accounts. If you do not mind receiving an occasional advertisement by email, or filling out a small questionnaire, this is a great way to save money. If you choose to do this,

be sure to reduce your service plan to an Internet-only plan. To find a free email account, simply use an Internet browser and type the words "Free Email".

Free Personal Web-Sites
Many Internet providers now offer free personal web-sites as an added incentive. The personal web sites usually include a maximum amount of megabytes and can be beneficial if you would like to maintain a web site.

Technical Support
Inquire of friends and family about the quality of the technical support that you expect to receive from a potential Internet provider.

TRAVELING BY AIR

Air travel can be quite expensive, but very convenient...at least some of the time. This section has been developed so that the frequent flier, as well as the not-so-frequent flier, can minimize the money spent on traveling, as well as fully understand and utilize their rights as a customer.

1. SAVING ON AIRLINE TICKETS

Advance Booking

Many airlines require tickets to be reserved at least fourteen (14) to twenty-one (21) days in advance in order to receive a discount.

Become A Courier

Shipping freight domestically and internationally can be very expensive. Because of this expense, certain airline freight companies will offer incentives to passengers willing to offer their luggage space on a flight or to carry-on a package. The incentives vary according to the situation. However, partially paid airfare or free travel is not uncommon.

To locate an airline freight company in your area, search the Internet, call the local freight office of airlines, or look in the yellow pages of the telephone book. To become a courier you may have to agree to a background check and sign several legal documents. However, the benefits may be worth the time involved in completing these tasks.

Check For Airfare Reductions

Sometimes airlines will honor reductions in airfares after a ticket has been issued, but only when the customer inquires about the reduction. Airfares can be discounted for several reasons, but the most common reason to reduce fares is to ensure the flight is fully booked. Therefore, it may be to your advantage to check for a reduction in airfare prior to your departure. If you do find there is a reduction in the airfare, contact the airline and request a refund of the difference.

Comparison Shop
As with any purchase, you should be aware of competitive prices. The same is true for airline tickets. Therefore, contact several airlines, a travel agent, and search the Internet to locate the best deal.

E-Mail Discount Notifications
Many of the major airlines now offer customers e-mail notices for discounted air travel. These discounts are usually for weekend travel, such as leaving on a Saturday and returning on a Tuesday or Wednesday. However, some of the e-mail notices are promotional rates to various cities the airline services.

To receive these notices, simply visit the airline's Internet web-site and register to be added to their mailing lists. Although, the airfare may be a bargain, you may have to be willing to have flexible plans and go on short notice.

Fare Wars
Because the airline industry is highly competitive, airlines will occasionally reduce their prices in order to obtain a larger market share. In order to retain customers, an airline will match or lower fares. This process creates what is known as a "fare war". Fare wars are usually announced through the news, but you can also contact airline reservation centers or travel agents about any current fare wars that may be occurring.

Flight Times & Locations
When searching for airline tickets, inquire about different days of the week for the departure or arrival of your flight. For instance, traveling during the midweek or on Saturdays will result in additional savings. Departing on a Tuesday, Wednesday, or a Saturday can also provide significant savings. In addition, research the discounts for departing or arriving during different times of the day or by including a Saturday night stay-over into your trip. Flying in the early morning or a late-night flight (red eye) can usually provide significant discounts as well. Check fares for flights with connections. These flights are often substantially less than direct flights; however, the amount of time to reach your destination can be increased

significantly. Finally, if you live in an area with more than one airport, inquire about airfares for each airport.

Package Deals
Depending on the airline and season, some airlines offer package deals that include airfare, hotel accommodations, and car rentals. Although these packages are commonly to off-peak areas, such as Florida during the summer, they are offered at significant price reductions. Because these package deals are offered infrequently and may go unannounced, be sure to inquire about them when booking your flight.

Tickets Purchased On The Internet
To reduce the overhead expense an airline must incur, airlines are now offering the ability for customers to access flight schedules and rates via the Internet. To promote the use of the Internet, airlines may provide significant discounts and various promotional programs. In addition, airlines may offer additional frequent flier miles when purchasing tickets through the Internet.

Travel Agents
A good travel agent can save you a significant amount of time and money. Travel agents are aware of fare wars, discount packages, and best of all, they have all the information available to them in a matter of minutes. Therefore, if you do not have the time to spend looking for the best deals, a good travel agent can save you a significant amount of time and money.

Because travel agents often work for commissions from the airlines, hotel and car rental industries, they do not charge for their services. However, if a travel agent charges a fee, it is usually a minimal charge.

Family Medical Emergencies/Deaths
If a family medical emergency or a death occurs and you must book a flight with almost no prior notice, mention to the airline sales representative your situation. Most airlines have agreements for reduced prices under extraneous circumstances and they should be able to meet your request with a discount. However, most airlines will require you to provide proof to them regarding the family medical emergency or death, such as a letter from a physician.

2. COMPLAINING TO AIRLINES

When traveling by air you want to get to your destination in a safe, inexpensive, and timely manner. Receiving anything else can be disappointing and quite frustrating, especially when you fail to receive compensation for your frustration.

Complaining to an airline is the same as complaining to any other company. Therefore, refer to the "Complaint Letters & Telephone Calls" section on page 28. Although many of the details you will need when complaining to an airline are included in the "Complaint Letters & Telephone Calls" section, below are some specific points to consider when complaining to an airline.

Complain At The Airport

The best use of your time, particularly when stuck in an airport due to airline problems, is to address your complaint while at the airport. If you are aware of your rights and you complain effectively, you are more likely to be provided immediate satisfaction.

Complaining By Mail Or Telephone

The "Complaint Letters & Telephone Calls" section will provide you the most effective methods to complaining by mail or telephone. However, when complaining to an airline, be sure to include the following information:

- State the problem, cities, dates of travel, flight numbers, and flight times.
- Include your name, address, telephone number, e-mail address and frequent flier number.
- If you fly the airline often, make the airline aware that you travel on their airline frequently.
- State the form of compensation that you are expecting (refer to the "Negotiating" section on page 86).
- Send a letter to the airline's customer service office at the airline's headquarters, as well as to the airline's customer service office at the location where your problem occurred. You can obtain these addresses from the Internet or by calling the airline's toll-free telephone number.

3. AIRLINE CUSTOMER RIGHTS

As an airline customer, you should be aware of your rights. Understanding and utilizing these rights will assist in making your travel experience more enjoyable.

Delayed Flights/Canceled Flights

Airlines are not required by federal law to compensate you for a delayed/canceled flight. However, most airlines have adopted their own policy for compensation for this situation. In most cases, delayed/canceled flights are caused by bad weather or air traffic delays. Compensation for these types of delays/cancellations is unlikely. However, compensation for delays/cancellations related to mechanical problems can be justified. To learn about your specific airline's delayed/canceled flight policy, request a copy of your ticket's contract from an airline customer service representative.

Getting Bumped

Airlines intentionally overbook flights in anticipation of individuals not arriving for scheduled flights. Furthermore, airlines overbook flights in order to maximize their flights, as it is cheaper to bump a passenger than to fly the plane with empty seats.

Many people consider the process of being bumped as a major inconvenience. Although at times it can be, in most cases it simply means delaying your arrival time to your destination by a few hours. In many cases, these few hours may be worth the benefits received from getting bumped.

For passengers with a flexible schedule, overbooking presents a rewarding opportunity. Some of the more common benefits you can earn when getting bumped include airline vouchers, free airline tickets, first-class upgrades, or several other miscellaneous services and products that are discussed in the "Airline Freebies & Lesser-Known Benefits" section on page 125.

Listed below are methods/situations that will increase your chances of being bumped.
- Book flights during the summer and other peak travel times (i.e. holidays) as they are often overbooked.

- Fly to popular destinations such as the Southwest and Southeast U.S. during the winter because they are often over booked.
- Request flights that are almost completely full, in order to increase your chances of being bumped.
- Make your reservations on smaller planes such as 727s and 737s.
- Arrive at the airport at least ninety (90) minutes prior to your flight's departure and request to be placed on the volunteer list for passengers willing to be bumped if necessary.
- Arrive at the boarding gate as early as possible and request to be placed on the volunteer list for passengers willing to be bumped if necessary.
- This list may be the same as the one you offered to be placed on when you checked in, but it allows the customer service personnel that are capable of offering the bump to place your name with your face. Therefore, be very polite when you visit with the customer service personnel and position yourself near the check-in gate. This will make you visible to the customer service personnel and keep them aware of your interests.
- When the customer service personnel requests volunteers do not delay in your response or you may miss your chance of getting bumped. Sit as close to the reservation desk as possible or stand at the side of the counter as this will allow you the ability to overhear the customer service personnel discussing possible announcements for volunteers. If they decide to ask for volunteers, volunteer yourself prior to them making an announcement on the intercom system.
- If you are flexible with your travel plans, place your name on the volunteer list. As other passengers arrive, your seat location will most likely be given away to accommodate other passengers wanting specific seating assignments. Thus, prior to departure, the only seats that remain available are those located in the first-class seating section. So instead of causing an over-crowding on the next flight, the customer service representative may place you on the airplane with a first-class seating assignment.
- If you are called upon as a volunteer to be bumped, only accept the bump if you are comfortable with the offer they are providing. However, before agreeing, request to be given a first-class seating assignment on the flight you are being bumped to. Also, depending on how long you will have to wait for the next flight, you may also ask for

several other items, such as food vouchers, calling cards, and reading materials.

Your Rights When Being Bumped

Listed below are your rights, as well as other forms of compensation you are eligible for as an airline customer should you volunteer to be, or are told that you are, getting bumped off your normal flight plan.

- No compensation is usually due to you if the airline is able to get you to your final destination within one hour of your original flight's arrival time.
- If you are delayed between one and two hours past your original flight's arrival time, you should be entitled to the lessor of the value of your one-way paid fare to a maximum of $200. This is a federally mandated amount enforced by the Department of Transportation.
- If you are delayed more than two hours, and the airline can not arrange a flight, you should be entitled to twice the value of your one-way paid fare up to a maximum of $400. This is also a federally mandated amount enforced by the Department of Transportation.
- If you must wait for more than two hours, ask for the following forms of compensation: free long distance calling cards (frequently offered in 5-minute intervals), a meal ticket, coupons for a free drink in flight, and free admission to the airline club.
- Although not a guarantee, you can ask for additional compensation for being bumped, such as a first-class upgrade. You are more likely to receive this type of compensation if the number of passengers bumped is small and you ask for an upgrade early.
- You can write to the airlines for additional compensation if you are unhappy with the ultimate results of your bumping.

Damaged, Missing & Lost Luggage

Occasionally when you travel luggage can be damaged, missing for a period of time, or lost and never found. In any of these situations you need to be aware of what to do to recover your losses.

Damaged Luggage

When traveling, be aware of the condition of your luggage. When you arrive at your destination, be sure to inspect any luggage that was checked for transportation. If damage has occurred, inform the airline of the damage before leaving the airport. Although this may be inconvenient, depending on the amount of damage to your luggage, receiving compensation can be worth the additional time spent at the airport.

In most cases, the airline will provide you some paperwork for you to take with you to process your claim. This will allow you to take your belongings home and return the damaged luggage to the airport at your convenience, usually within a certain time period. The airline will most likely offer two solutions: either repair the damage or replace the luggage with an equivalently or higher priced piece of luggage.

Missing Luggage

If your luggage is missing when you arrive at your final destination you should contact the airline immediately and fill out the appropriate paperwork while at the airport. Be sure to retain a copy of all the paperwork you fill out and be as specific as possible regarding the contents and description of your luggage. Also, before leaving the airport, be sure you are aware of the lost luggage process and have contact telephone numbers for the airline.

Compensation for missing luggage is difficult to receive. However, depending on the airline, you can request a cash advance from the airline in order to purchase clothes or other personal items needed for your trip until your luggage is found and returned to you. In addition, you may be eligible to receive compensation based on the number of days that your luggage is missing.

Lost Luggage

If you have not received your luggage by the time period that the airline promised, be sure to contact the airline immediately. After a certain time period, specific to each airline, your luggage will be determined to be lost. If you were flying a connection flight, the airline that was used to get you to your final destination is responsible for your missing or lost luggage. In most cases, the paperwork you filled out when your luggage was missing will be used as the basis for compensation. Therefore, be detailed with the contents and description of your lost luggage.

To assist in the compensation process, the airline may require that you provide receipts or other evidence of the value of the contents that is in the lost luggage. If you do not have detailed records of the contents and their prices, you will have to bargain with the airline over the value of the contents of the lost luggage.

Damaged Personal Belongings

Occasionally damage can occur to the contents of your luggage. Receiving compensation for such damages is very unlikely, unless the luggage is obviously damaged as well. If your luggage is damaged, refer to the "Damaged Luggage" section above. If on the other hand, your luggage is not damaged, your options are primarily limited to complaint letters and/or telephone calls. To learn more about how to write a complaint letter or make a complaint telephone call, refer to the "Complaint Letter & Telephone Calls" section on page 28.

Compensation For Damaged, Missing, Or Lost Luggage

Be aware that if your luggage is damaged, missing, or lost on a domestic flight the maximum compensation that you can receive is usually $1,250. Also, if your luggage is damaged, missing, or lost on an international flight the maximum compensation that your can receive is usually based on the weight of your luggage. To learn more about compensation for luggage that is damaged, missing, or lost by the airline you are traveling with, contact the airline's customer service center.

4. AIRLINE FREEBIES & LESSER-KNOWN BENEFITS

Airlines offer a variety of free services and products as devices to satisfy their customers. These services and products are usually only offered as needed, such as when a customer is complaining. However, this section will describe some of these services and products and inform you how to get them without complaining.

First-Class Upgrades

In some situations, airlines will ask certain passengers to change seats in order to accommodate a passenger that needs assistance with their seating. The most accommodating location is the aisle seats in the first row of coach seats, which are located directly behind the first-class section. This row of seats is commonly referred to as the bulkhead row. Therefore, when making your reservation, request one of the aisle seats in this row.

As other passengers arrive, even if the plane is not full, passengers will request special seating needs, such as assistance entering and exiting a plane.   To accommodate these customers, the customer service representative may call upon you to provide your seat to the other passenger. When this happens, particularly if the person needing assistance is traveling with another person, your chances for a first-class upgrade are good. State to the customer service representative that you would be happy to offer your seat, but you would like a seat with a similar location (leg room and aisle location). If there are no other locations available in the coach seating that meet your requirements, subtly suggest that you would be willing to accept an upgrade to first class. In this case, the customer service representative may be more likely to place you in first-class seating than the person needing assistance, as the person needing assistance may have another person traveling with them.

Magazines & Newspapers
Airlines purchase magazines and newspapers in bulk quantities to provide to customers as reading material while traveling. Often these magazines and newspapers are placed in the first-class section of the airplane so that the first-class customers have access to them first. However, on many flights, the flight attendants fail to inform passengers that magazine and newspapers are available. Therefore, when boarding the airplane, request that the flight attendant direct you to their magazine and newspaper selection.

Free Calling Cards
Many major airlines have calling cards they offer to customers. These calling cards are frequently in five-minute increments and are provided to customers upon request, particularly if there is a specific need for the calling card. Therefore, if your plane is delayed, go to the airline's customer service desk and inquire about a free calling card. In many cases, the customer service representative will have a large stack of calling cards available and will just hand you a few of them.

Free Alcoholic Beverages
A common practice of major airlines is to offer free drinks to passengers when a flight has been delayed. Although this benefit is not announced on the intercom system during the flight, the best way to determine if you can receive free alcoholic drinks is to simply ask the flight attendant how much the alcoholic beverages are. If they are offering them for free, they will inform you that there is no charge. However, if they offer you a price, simply decline and request another beverage if you choose.

Alcoholic Beverage Coupons

Because of the difficulty of providing passengers change for alcoholic beverages during flights, many airlines are offering customers the ability to purchase books of coupons that can be used to purchase alcoholic beverages during a flight. These coupon books are usually available at the customer service desk and are discounted to provide passengers an incentive to purchase them.

Airline Travel Vouchers

Vouchers for airline travel are a great incentive and can be quite valuable, but beware! Vouchers do have limitations, such as expiration dates, blackout dates, and may not be transferable.

Listed below are common aspects of vouchers to consider before agreeing to accept a voucher in exchange for your seat on a flight or for some other service you provide.

- Vouchers are usually valid for one year from date of issuance. However, keep in mind that the flight only has to be booked within one year. The actual flight can take place after one year.
- Vouchers usually have blackout dates associated with them. For instance most vouchers have blackout dates that will include New Year's, Thanksgiving and Christmas. However, there are vouchers that do no have blackout dates.
- Most vouchers are non-transferable. However, some vouchers allow you to transfer the voucher to a relative or a friend as an added benefit.
- Some vouchers can only be redeemed at an airline ticket counter or through a travel agent. However, travel agents cannot provide change for a voucher, nor can they create a new voucher if the voucher is for a value higher than the ticket being purchased (i.e. the voucher is worth $250 and the flight costs $185).
- To avoid losing the value of a voucher, some airlines allow customers to mail the voucher to them in order to purchase lower-valued tickets. They will return the ticket and a new voucher for the remaining amount. If you decide to use this option, be sure to have the voucher insured and use a return receipt in case the voucher is lost in the mail.

5. FREQUENT FLIER MILES & PROGRAMS

Frequent flier programs allow frequent travelers to earn free trips, upgrades, and other awards. Below are various tips regarding frequent flier miles in order to earn these valuable travel perks as quickly as possible.

Selecting A Frequent Flyer Program

The most common method of selecting a frequent flier program is by flying regularly with an airline that either offers the lowest fares or an airline that offers the best flight schedule. However, there are other factors to consider when selecting a frequent flier program. Below are questions and factors to consider when choosing a frequent flier program.

- Does the airline fly to your desired destinations? For instance, if you are earning miles to eventually fly to the Caribbean for a dream vacation and the airline does not fly to that destination.
- Will the frequent flyer program's miles expire? If the miles do eventually expire, how long are they good for?
- Compare blackout periods and expirations to other frequent flier programs.
- Inquire about the ability to transfer free trips, upgrades, and other awards to immediate family members.
- Research the number of partners (other airlines, rental car companies, and hotels) that the frequent flyer program is associated with.
- Does the airline have a minimum frequent flyer mileage award for each trip taken? For instance, some airlines will credit your account for 500 miles even though your one-way flight was only 300 miles.
- Determine the mileage or trips required each year to earn certain airline privileges (i.e. earn double miles, etc.) through elite programs.

Maximizing Your Frequent Flyer Miles

Frequent flier miles can be earned in a number of ways. Learning how to maximize frequent flier mileage will allow you to reap the benefits of the program more quickly. Listed below are suggestions to maximize your frequent flier program.

- Select one frequent flyer program and utilize that airline as much as possible to accumulate frequent flyer miles.
- Strive to become an elite status with your selected frequent flier program. An elite status is usually earned by accumulating a certain fixed number of miles or traveling on a specific number of flights per

year. Many programs use 25,000, 50,000, and 100,000 miles as the measurements to achieve an elite status. Based on the status that you acquire and the airline's frequent flier program, you can earn significant benefits as an elite level member. For example, many of the major airlines allow elite members to earn double miles for flights they take. However, miles in this calculation are only for true miles flown and not for miles earned through other methods.

- If at the end of the year, you are close to earning an elite status with a frequent flyer program, consider taking steps to earn the additional mileage before year-end, such as purchasing an inexpensive weekend flight. This effort can provide you extremely valuable benefits the following year.

- Become familiar with frequent flyer program partners, including hotels, rental car companies, cruise-lines, vacation package companies, long-distance phone companies, as well as a whole host of other companies.

- Read all of the airline's frequent flier newsletters or flyers that you receive, as they will inform you of any changes to the program and any upcoming promotions.

- Inquire about a frequent flyer program credit card. Be sure to consider the expense of the annual fee and the time required to earn a free flight from the credit card. For instance, if you only charge about $5,000 to your credit card each year, it will take you 5 years as well as 5 years of annual fees to earn a free flight ($5,000 X 5 years = 25,000 miles).

- Consider purchasing airline tickets on the Internet, as many frequent flyer programs now offer participants bonus miles for using this option.

- If your frequent flier mileage is about to expire, you may want to book a flight prior to the expiration date even if you do not have a tentative date. The expense of paying for changes to the flight (approximately $50 to $75) is worth retaining the frequent flyer miles. Also, you have an additional year to use that ticket before it expires.

- Retain all receipts and ticket stubs for air travel you have taken in case your mileage is not credited properly, as documentation of your flight is needed in order to receive credit for mileage.

- Review your frequent flyer miles frequently to minimize lost mileage due to expiration dates or changes in frequent flyer programs.

UTILITIES

Every month, one of the most unpredictable expenses is for utilities. Gas, electricity, and water are often very difficult to monitor and make it extremely difficult to create an efficient monthly/yearly budget. Although the use of your utilities will vary season to season, after living in a residence long enough, you begin to develop an average usage. Regardless if you are in a new residence or have been living in your current residence for several years, this section will provide you a number of suggestions and ideas to implement in order to check for mistakes and to reduce your monthly utility expense.

1. CHECKING THE BILL FOR MISTAKES

Checking your monthly utility bill is a good way to determine if there are mistakes in your billing. For example, mistakes can occur if a number on your meter is read incorrectly by the meter-reader or if the rate calculation is done improperly. If there is a discrepancy between the meter numbers on your billing and the numbers you read on your meter, or if the rate calculation is incorrect, contact your utility provider to correct the mistake.

2. AIR CONDITIONING & HEATING

Air conditioning and heating are usually the primary users of power. Listed below are suggestions to reduce the amount of power used by air conditioners and heaters.

- Typically, the most beneficial setting for your heating/air-conditioning fan is "auto". The "auto" setting is more efficient than switching from the "on" and "off" position.
- Set the air conditioner to 78 degrees Fahrenheit during the summer months and the heater to 70 degrees Fahrenheit during the winter months.

- Investigate purchasing a digital thermostat with a timer. These thermostats can be programmed to turn the temperature up/down during certain times of the day, thus saving a considerable amount of money. For example, you can program your heater to maintain a temperature of 65 degrees Fahrenheit between the hours of 11:00 P.M. to 6:00 A.M. and then return to 70 degrees while you are preparing yourself for the day from 6:00 A.M. to 8:00 A.M. Furthermore, you can then reduce the temperature to 60 degrees from 8:00 A.M. to 5:00 P.M. since no one will be in the residence during these hours.

- If you do not have a digital thermostat with a timer, consider turning off your heat/air-conditioning during periods of time you will be away for several hours, such as the time you are at work. However, during the winter months, consider turning your thermostat to a lower temperature, such as 50 to 60 degrees Fahrenheit to avoid causing your water pipes from freezing.

- Keep items that give off heat, such as televisions, stereos, computer equipment and lights away from your thermostat as it could misread the correct air temperature within the residence.

- When you first set your thermostat, avoid setting it at very extreme temperatures (above normal) expecting the house to cool/heat more quickly. By setting the thermostat to extreme temperatures, you will cause your heating/air-conditioning unit to work harder, thus creating a higher utility bill.

- Request a home-energy audit to be performed by your electric or gas utility company. These services are often provided free of charge or for a reasonable amount of money. An audit can identify and provide suggestions on methods to save a few hundred dollars per year on your heating/air-conditioning expense. In fact, most utility companies offer rebates and other incentives for making your home more energy efficient.

- During the winter months, let direct sunlight into your residence in order to assist with the heating process. During the summer months, block direct sunlight from entering your house to assist with the cooling process.

- Keep furniture, drapes, or other home accessories from blocking vents in your residence. The placements of vents, particularly in newer homes, were determined for the most effective and efficient heating and cooling process.

- If there are rooms in your home that are not occupied, close the door and heating/air-conditioning vents in those rooms to conserve power.
- Research the expense of installing ceiling fans. These will help circulate the cool/hot air, thus avoiding cooler air from settling and warmer air from rising. This will allow the thermostat to reflect a "true" reading of the air temperature in the residence.
- Purchase vent covers and flow-directors. Vent covers can be used to effectively close a vent that is not being used. These are usually made of a magnetic material and can be placed over the entire vent. The vent flow-directors are ¼ inch circle covers that can be placed on the vent to direct the flow of the exiting air in a certain direction. For example, during the winter months, to keep warmer air from rising faster, face the vent flow-director down. During summer months, turn the vent flow director in the opposite direction to keep cooler air from settling on the lower half of the home. Both the vent cover and vent flow-directors can be found at a hardware or home improvement store.
- Change the filters on your heater/air-conditioner monthly during regular-use months and as needed during the rest of the year. This will enable air to flow into the system more effectively and allows the system to use less energy.
- If you are living in a residence that has wall-mounted heater/air-conditioner units, consider arranging your residence in an effective means to reduce your use of energy. For example, if you spend a considerable amount of time on the computer or television when at home, consider placing the computer or television in an area where the heater/air-conditioner units are located.
- If you only have a wall-mounted air-conditioning unit in one area of your home, such as the living room, consider purchasing an additional unit to use in your bedroom instead of constantly using the one unit in the living room to cool the entire residence.

3. LIGHTING

Lighting can be a significant use of power. Listed below are suggestions to reduce the amount of power used by lights in your home.

- Turn off all unused lights.
- Instead of turning on several lights in a room in order to read or work, consider rearranging lamps, or purchasing a lamp to place in the area you are working.

- Exchange on/off switches with dimmer switches in rooms where full lighting may not always be needed, such as the dining room. Dimmer switches regulate the amount of energy that is sent to the light fixture, thus conserving energy.
- Utilize light-colored floors, ceiling, blinds/curtains, and walls to reduce the need for lighting.
- Purchase low-wattage light bulbs or energy-efficient fluorescent lighting.
- Clean light fixtures on a regular basis to prevent the accumulation of dust on the fixture and bulbs.
- Many light fixtures in apartments and older homes are inefficient at spreading light. Therefore, consider purchasing new fixtures to better incorporate light into a room, and reduce the need for multiple lighting devices.

4. APPLIANCES

Appliances can use an incredible amount of power. The suggestions listed below can assist in reducing the amount of power used by appliances in your home.

- When heating food, such as leftover pizza, only pre-heat the oven for a few minutes (3 to 5), prior to placing your food in the oven.
- A clothes dryer requires a large amount of power. Therefore, consider hanging your clothes outside to dry during the summer months or inside during the winter months. In addition, avoiding the use of a clothes dryer will help your clothes last longer, since dryers can cause clothing to shrink and wear quickly.
- When using a clothes dryer, dry loads of clothes in sequence. This will allow other loads to benefit from the heat generated during previous loads.
- When using a washing machine or dishwasher, wash full loads. If you must wash a smaller load, set your water level lower.
- Attempt to wash clothes in cold water as much as possible. This will reduce the expense of heating the water.
- Utilize your microwave oven as much as possible, instead of using a traditional oven, as microwaves are more energy efficient.
- A freezer should be just over three-quarters full capacity for optimum efficiency. If your freezer is less than three-quarters full, fill up some empty milk cartons or containers with water to take up the empty space.

The energy released from these containers will assist in maintaining the temperature in the freezer, thus reducing the need to constantly have the freezer run. If your freezer is over three-quarters capacity, consider removing items or rearranging them to maximize space.

- Keep items in your freezer away from the cooling vents. These vents are used to maintain the temperature in the freezer. By keeping items away from the vents, the freezer is allowed to work effectively.
- When cooking, cover your pots and containers to conserve the heat.
- Only place room-cooled containers and food into the refrigerator or freezer. These will take less energy to cool versus warm or hot containers of food.
- When placing new ice trays into the freezer, fill them with cold water.
- When cooking in the oven, avoid continually opening the door, as this will only allow heat to escape.
- If using a dishwasher, avoid using the drying cycle and simply crack open the door and allow the dishes to air dry.
- Dust and debris can cause an appliance to work ineffectively. Therefore, be sure to clean your appliances on a regular basis. Listed below are a few suggestions.
  1. *Refrigerator* - Clean the inside vents of debris, vacuum dust from underneath the unit, and clean dust from the back of the unit at least once a year or as needed.
  2. *Range* - Clean debris from the oven compartments and stove heating element as needed.
  3. *Clothes Dryer* - By cleaning the ventilation chamber, you can cut the drying time in half. Therefore, clean lint from the lint screen after every load of clothing that is dried. Clear the main dryer vent to the outside at least once a year, as lint will accumulate where the vent turns or curves. If your dryer ventilation tube is partially located behind a wall, consider hiring a chimney sweep to clean the vent or use a long wire to break up larger pieces of lint from the vent. This should be performed every 5 to 10 years. If you are renting an older apartment, request that the vents be cleaned as part of your move-in negotiation.
  4. *Washing Machine* - Never let your washing machine sit unused for long periods of time as several components are made of plastic. Over time these components may dry out and become brittle.

Also, be sure all water-intake hoses are free from kinks. This will allow the washing machine to work more efficiently.

5. *Dish Washer* - Clean the water filter inside the dishwasher of food and debris particles as needed. To determine if your dishwasher has a filter system, review your owner's manual.

5. WATER

By implementing a few of the suggestions below, you can cause a significant reduction in the amount of water used in your home.

- Purchase a water-efficient showerhead. These can reduce your water usage by one-third.
- If you have any leaky faucets, fix them or have them fixed immediately. Over several months, a slow drip can equal several gallons of wasted water. Most often, correcting the problem will usually only involve changing the washer or tightening a valve.
- When using your garbage disposal, use cold water rather than hot water.
- If your toilet slowly loses water from its holding tank (when the holding tank refills without being flushed), consider purchasing a new holding tank plunger kit. They are very inexpensive and can be easily installed. Also, they are an effective way to save a considerable amount of water every year.
- Many holding tanks, especially on older toilets, are quite large. Therefore, every time you flush the toilet, a considerable amount of water is used. To reduce the amount of water, consider adding items to the holding tank to take up space, such as rocks. To avoid having items being pulled into the holding tank drainage hole, be sure the items you use to fill space are larger than the drainage hole and heavy enough to stay in a specific location (usually items larger than a fist are sufficient).
- Contact your water company to have a water-usage audit performed on your home.

6. OTHER CONSIDERATIONS

- Seal windows and doors that you do not use.
- Add/replace insulation, weather-strip, or caulk to outside walls, the attic, doors, windows, and the basement.

WAREHOUSE CLUBS

Warehouse clubs are large retail outlets, commonly located in warehouse-structured buildings, which sell a variety of items packaged in bulk quantities and often a few high-priced items. Overall, these items will be sold at considerably discounted prices (when comparing them based on "price-per-item" to a non-warehouse club store).   The price difference occurs because of several factors. The largest factor is the low overhead the warehouse clubs have to run and maintain their facilities, such as little or no advertising. Another factor is that warehouse clubs can purchase items in significant quantities.   This allows them to re-sell these items to their customers for significant savings, while they still retain a portion of the difference in price for profit. Regardless of how the savings are created, warehouse clubs, if effectively used, can create significant savings for customers.

1. WHAT DO WAREHOUSE CLUBS SELL?

Warehouse clubs sell a tremendous variety of items. However, particular brand name items and quantities do vary. For example, you may see your favorite brand of toothpaste for sale at a local warehouse club for several weeks, and then all of a sudden they may not carry that brand for several months. This situation is simply due to the supply of that product and the ability of the warehouse club's purchasing agents to purchase particular items at reasonable prices.

Listed below are samples of items commonly available at warehouse clubs:

- Food
- Pet products
- Electronics
- Household products
- Furniture
- Paper products
- Automobile products
- Clothes
- Health products
- Eyeglasses
- Other items (books, plants, sporting goods, office supplies, sunglasses, etc.)

2. MEMBERSHIP

Do not assume that in order to become a member of a warehouse club you have to meet some specific criteria. Although in some cases this may be true, for the most part anyone can join. Membership usually only involves filling out a membership application, paying the membership annual fee, and having a card made with your picture on it.

Annual membership fees are usually between $30 and $40 and usually include membership for the spouse. In addition, some warehouse clubs allow you to add up to three guests onto your annual membership for about half the price of normal membership fees. For example, if you and three friends decide to open a warehouse club membership account together, and the membership fee for one member is $30, you and your friends could obtain membership to that warehouse club for $75 ($30 x 1 and $15 x 3). Thus, splitting the annual membership fees between you and three friends equally will reduce your annual membership expense.

3. IS IT WORTH THE ANNUAL PAYMENT?

To determine if joining a warehouse club is worth the expense, consider your current purchasing habits and potential upcoming purchases. For example, if you are living by yourself and do not intend to purchase any high-valued items, a membership may not be cost effective. However, if you are living with another person, or several other people, plan on purchasing several higher-priced items (such as new tires, couch, computer, or appliance) in the near future, a membership may be cost effective. To be sure if a membership will be cost effective or not, consider visiting the warehouse club to see what particular items they tend to offer customers, and see if those items fit your needs.

4. ONE-DAY VISITOR PASSES

Many warehouse clubs will allow you to shop at their store by using a one-day visitor pass. This will allow you to browse through the store and determine if a membership to that warehouse club is worth your investment. These passes may also allow you, if you choose to not become a member, to purchase items from the warehouse club for a small charge. To obtain a one-day visitor pass ask a warehouse club customer-service representative once you enter the club. Revisit the warehouse club for additional one-day visitor passes if necessary.

5. REBATE PROGRAMS

A nice benefit that some warehouse clubs offer their customers is rebate programs. Different rebate offers will be advertised each month. These rebate programs usually increase your savings considerably. One of the best parts of a rebate program with a warehouse club is that many warehouse clubs offer their customers a rebate center. Rebate centers allow customers to send all rebate materials to one location and receive one reimbursement check conveniently and easily.

6. COUPONS

Warehouse clubs do not commonly accept manufacturer coupons. This is because of the overhead expense the warehouse club would incur to maintain a coupon program and because of the pre-existing savings on the items sold at their locations.

7. OTHER MEMBER BENEFITS

In addition to the items mentioned throughout this section, warehouse clubs also offer their customers a variety of services. The following are a sample of these services:

- Long-distance telephone programs
- Internet service
- Pre-printed checks
- Travel and Vacation packages
- Vehicle purchase programs
- Mortgage services
- Insurance policies
- Extended warranties

WEDDINGS

Your wedding day is supposed to be one of the happiest and most joyous occasions of your life. For many people, this means the wedding must also be one of the most expensive experiences of their life, but that is not always true. Although eloping is an inexpensive method of getting married, following a few of the suggestions discussed below can lead to an extravagant wedding on a reasonable budget.

Although there are a number of excellent books, magazines, and web-sites that offer additional suggestions on timing and organizing a wedding, the suggestions listed below are somewhat different. These suggestions offer methods that most individuals can implement in order to cut costs and save a significant amount of money on every aspect of a wedding.

1. TIMING OF THE WEDDING
Determining the timing of your wedding as early as possible is important. Listed below are a few suggestions to consider when determining the timing of your wedding.

- Try and avoid a Saturday-night wedding, as this is the most popular time to have a wedding. Instead have either an early Saturday-afternoon wedding or a Friday-night wedding.
- Schedule your wedding in months other than May, June, September, and October. These months are the most popular and therefore have premiums associated with their cost because of demand. In addition, it is usually more difficult to bargain with the reception hall if they can book the dates easily with another wedding party.
- Try not to schedule your wedding close to a major holiday. Not only will you be competing for the location with other wedding parties, but

companies and organizations are in need of locations in which to have their holiday celebrations during those same times.

2. BUDGETING

When you have determined the date of your wedding, it is important to budget your time and expenses to prepare for the big day. Again, there are many resources available that can provide further information about the proper timing of various aspects of the wedding. The suggestions below are methods to help with the budgeting process.

- Make a calendar that includes at least six months prior to your wedding date. Dedicate this calendar to be used only for wedding planning. As you determine when certain aspects of the wedding need to be completed, be sure to mark those dates on your calendar. For example, if it is suggested to reserve the photographer at least four months prior to your wedding date, mark that on your calendar and be sure to have it completed by that date.

- Create a wedding planner to store and record all of your wedding information. For instance, utilize a binder, notebook, or a computer.

- Develop a financial budget for your wedding and stick to it! Take into account the amount you can afford to spend as well as any amount your family intends to contribute. If your family intends to help, ask them to be specific. For example, are they going to contribute money, or will they provide a certain aspect of the wedding, such as the rehearsal dinner? When calculating the financial budget, be sure to consider such items as tax and gratuities as they can add up quickly. Financial gifts can also be considered, although it is not recommended. However, if you decide to include this as a part of your financial budget, be sure to use a conservative estimate.

- Assign duties to responsible family and friends. Once you decide on how you want to have a certain function at the rehearsal dinner, wedding, or reception completed, ask various people to be in charge of making sure that function is accomplished. By doing this, you will relieve yourself of unwanted stress and make people feel as if they are needed

3. LOCATION OF THE REHEARSAL DINNER, WEDDING & RECEPTION

There are a number of locations available to have a rehearsal dinner, wedding, or reception. Listed below are a few suggestions to consider.

- Depending on your religion, churches and synagogues are good places to start looking. Churches and synagogues are nice options because they are usually very inexpensive. However, unless you are able to lock in your date early, church wedding schedules will fill up very quickly. Therefore, you will need to reserve these well in advance.

- Consider having your rehearsal dinner, wedding, and reception at a private facility, such as an Elks lodge, Moose lodge, or VFW hall. Some of these locations also have outdoor gazebos that can be used for an outdoor wedding, and then the building can be used as the reception area. Many of these facilities also provide catering services.

- Public areas are a great idea for a rehearsal dinner, such as using a reserved spot in a city park for an outside barbecue rehearsal dinner. Also, state and local governments will rent out recreational facilities as a location to have a reception.

- Consider using a family or friend's home as a location for these functions.

4. REGISTERING FOR GIFTS

When registering for wedding gifts, select them based on your need. For example, if neither you nor your future spouse have many household belongings and have just started living on your own, you might consider registering for the more reasonably priced items. This will ensure that you will probably receive all of, or at least most of, the essential items you will need. Then you will not have to spend the money you receive as a wedding gift on purchasing a lot of small items for your new home.

Also, consider registering at a store that is located nationally, or at least in geographic areas where you are expecting people to purchase your gifts from. Also try to limit the number of stores you register at. This will again ensure that you receive most of, if not all of, the gifts you registered for. It also makes it easier to return or exchange gifts. You may also want to register at a store that is less "pricey".

5. INVITATIONS

Before purchasing invitations, compare prices from wedding stores, mail-order companies, local printing companies, and copy centers. Many of these locations have a wide selection of choices, and many often carry the same styles. If you are planning for a detailed and expensive reception (such as serving dinner), consider placing stamps on the RSVP. The small expense of including the postage for the return of the RSVP can play a major role in determining the amount of food to order. You may want to include a small note with the invitation requesting that people RSVP by telephone or email in order to prevent having to pay the return postage.

6. CLOTHING

Clothing for a wedding can be very expensive. Listed below are suggestions to reduce the expense of wedding clothes.

- Have the bridal party purchase their own dresses. When selecting their dresses, try to select an item that they can wear again. This may help to eliminate any resentment that the bridal party may have.
- Have the groom's wedding party rent their own tuxedos. On many occasions a large enough party will result in the groom's tuxedo for free.
- Consider having the groom's wedding party purchase pants and shirts similar in style to the groom's attire, instead of renting. Then rent cumberbuns and bow ties to complement the attire of the bride's wedding party. Some department stores will offer discounts when purchasing a large quantity of a certain item, such as dress shirts and pants.
- Rent a wedding dress from a rental shop or purchase one from a discount department store, consignment shop, or outlet store. Also review the classified section of your newspaper, as many people sell wedding dresses they have recently used or did not end up using. Other options are to use either your mother's or a friend's wedding dress and pay the small expense of having alterations made.

7. MAKE-UP & HAIR

Everyone wants to look their best on the wedding day. Listed below are suggestions to consider in order to reduce the costs associated with make-up and hair expenses.

- Ask a make-up consultant to assist with the bride's and her wedding party's make-up the day of the wedding. Many consultants are pleased to offer this service in hopes of obtaining future make-up sales. The bride may be able to receive a discount if she has a large wedding party.
- Have a local hairdresser (preferably a friend) prepare the bride's wedding party's hair the day of the wedding. This service can be obtained for a significant discount by arranging for the whole party to come in at once or by following some of the suggestions listed in the "Marketing at Your Wedding" section on page 147.

8. MUSIC

If you want to have live music played during the wedding and/or reception, contact local churches and synagogues or college music departments and ask for recommendations. You can usually receive these services for significant discounts compared to professional musicians. If you are planning to have dancing at your reception, you may want to consider hiring a disc jockey instead of a live band. Disc jockeys can offer a wider arrangement of music and often at a fraction of the expense of a band, usually $300-$500 compared to a band that can cost upwards of $1500 - $5000. (See the "Marketing at Your Wedding" section on page 147 for ways to receive discounts on this service.)

If the wedding and reception will be small, consider having a friend coordinate the music on a home-stereo system set up at the wedding and reception location. You can also request that people bring copies of their favorite music to add diversity to the styles of music offered.

9. PHOTOGRAPHY

Of all the details of the wedding, besides your memories, the photographs are something that can be treasured well after the wedding is over. Most wedding guides and planners suggest budgeting the largest amount of your wedding expense to your photographs because of the personal value they offer. This section offers methods to get great pictures, and a lot of them, without spending an arm and a leg for them.

- If using a professional photographer, consider offering some of the suggestions in the "Marketing at Your Wedding" section on page 147. These suggestions may provide you a significant discount in the fee.

- Request that friends with nice cameras take several roles of pictures for you before, during and after the ceremony. Offer people different types of film such as color and black & white film to diversify your collection of pictures.

- Contact local college art/photography departments, as well as local photo shops, and ask for recommendations of people that may be interested in being hired to take pictures.

- Place disposable cameras on each table along with a note asking guests to assist in taking pictures at the reception. This will provide you with quite a diverse variety of pictures. Also be sure to have a basket or decorated box available at the door for people to place the cameras in on their way out. It may also be wise to add a message on the camera as to where guests can leave the camera once they are finished. The official disposable wedding cameras with all the fancy markings on them are often more expensive. Therefore, you may want to buy regular disposable cameras in a large quantity at a wholesale club and decorate them yourself with wrapping paper and bows.

10. TRANSPORTATION

Using a nice car or limousine as the primary transportation for the bride and groom is a nice benefit that can make the wedding seem extra special. Below are ways to get this extra special touch for your wedding without much of an "extra" expense.

- Ask a family member or friend with a nice car to act as your chauffeur.

- Call a local car dealer and visit with the owner about arranging for one of their cars to be used as transportation during the wedding ceremonies. They will be more interested if you suggest that they can have the car available for people to look at during the ceremony. (For more information about receiving this service for free, read the section "Marketing at Your Wedding" located on page 147).

- Contact local funeral homes. Although this may sound gruesome, some funeral homes do use their limousines for functions during the evenings. Some also offer the use of the car for free in hopes that you will remember to think of them when deciding on, or offering suggestions to others, for funeral home services. However, you may be required to pay for the services of the driver.

11. REHEARSAL DINNER

A rehearsal dinner does not have to be extravagant. On many occasions, the guests are more interested in visiting with family and friends than they are in the food that is served. Listed below are suggestions to save money and have a great rehearsal dinner.

- As suggested in the "Location of the Rehearsal Dinner, Wedding, and Reception" section, consider having the dinner at a public park. If you decide to have a family member or friend cook, be sure to keep the menu simple so that everyone can be involved. Better yet, purchase a variety of ready-made food and serve it on disposable containers so that preparation and clean up are easy.
- Have the rehearsal dinner at a fun restaurant that caters to groups and can provide your group a help-yourself food buffet. This will enable you to control the expense of the food.
- Instead of calling the function a rehearsal dinner, call it a rehearsal get together, and offer a variety of snack foods instead of a full meal.
- Avoid providing alcoholic beverages as they can add a large expense to your overall wedding. If you choose to have alcohol, consider purchasing it in bulk, such as a keg, and designate someone to maintain it. You can also consider offering a cash bar.

12. RECEPTION

After the wedding ceremony, it is nice to offer your guests food and drinks at the reception. However, as mentioned in the "Rehearsal Dinner" section above, this function does not need to be expensive in order to be successful. This is a time when your guests are interested in visiting with family and friends and congratulating you. Consider some of the suggestions below for your reception.

- Provide the basics, such as a variety of snack foods, cake, and drinks. This is common for morning and early afternoon weddings.
- If the reception location caters food, try to negotiate the price by considering some of the suggestions in "Marketing at Your Wedding" section on page 147.
- Have family members and friends prepare food and/or snacks.
- As suggested in the section above, avoid purchasing alcoholic beverages.

13. WEDDING CAKE

The wedding cake is a treasured part of the wedding celebration. However, once it is all cut-up, and people are eating it, no one remembers what it looked like. Therefore, consider some of these suggestions.

- Purchase a small wedding cake. Once that is cut and dispersed, start using decorated sheet cakes. To hide the fact you are doing this, once the cake is cut by the bride and groom, have the cake taken away to be cut and bring out slices of both the wedding and sheet cake.
- Consider having a friend or family member make your wedding cake or the additional sheet cakes.
- Contact a local college and visit with the home economics department for recommendations of students wanting to earn extra money by making your cake.
- If purchasing the cake from a professional decorator, consider the suggestions in "Marketing at Your Wedding" section on page 147 as methods to reduce your expense.

14. DECORATIONS

Decorations can add a lot to the overall wedding celebration. Creativity is a major contributor to cutting the expense of decorations. Below are a few suggestions to consider.

- Have a local high school or college art or home economics group create decorations for you. In return, you can make a donation to their club for their work.
- Purchase live or fake plants that can be used in your new home as decorations or centerpieces. You can make them even more decorative by placing white lights on the plants.
- Use inexpensive glitter, candles, and ribbon bows as accents for tables.
- Reuse flowers from the wedding ceremony in your reception. Be sure to arrange to have a responsible friend or family member complete this task for you.
- Search rental stores or thrift shops for inexpensive decorations to use.

15. FLOWERS

Flowers are a beautiful accent to a wedding. However, once the celebration is over, those expensive flowers are no longer of use. Consider some of these suggestions to reduce the expense of your flowers.

- Contact a local high school or college horticulture group to prepare flowers for you. In return, you can make a donation to the club for their assistance.
- If purchasing flowers, get price comparisons from several florists as well as the floral section of your local supermarket. You can also use the suggestions listed in the "Marketing at Your Wedding" section located on page 147.
- Implement the use of silk, dried, and real flowers together in bouquets and boutonnieres.
- You can easily create your own centerpiece or bouquet by purchasing a book on flower arrangements.

16. GIFTS FOR THE WEDDING PARTY

Purchasing gifts for the wedding party is a token of appreciation for their help and friendship. It is also a nice thought, especially if you had the wedding party purchase or rent their own attire for your wedding. Although the gifts you choose are a personal choice, below are suggestions to consider when purchasing the gifts.

- Purchase the same gift for the whole wedding party in order to receive a discount.
- Pre-plan your purchase in order to purchase the gifts on sale.
- Make your own gifts, such as personalized photo albums of you and your wedding party.

17. HONEYMOON

Where you go on your honeymoon will be a factor of the remainder of your wedding budget. There are several sections located in this book that can assist in planning a great honeymoon on a limited budget, such as: the "Hotels" section on page 65, the "Rental Cars" section on page 99, and the "Traveling By Air" section on page 117.

18. MARKETING AT YOUR WEDDING

Marketing at your wedding is a simple and easy way to help reduce your expenses. What you are doing is simply negotiating with a service provider for a reduced rate on their services in exchange for some advertising.

Many of the services you will incorporate into your wedding build their businesses from recommendations. For example, the florists and photographers you contacted were probably referred to you from someone you knew or from someone that had used them.

The negotiation is simple. Simply ask the service provider if they will provide you a discount on their services in exchange for advertising at your wedding. Since this is not a common request for many of these service providers, they may want more information about what you are suggesting. State that you would be willing to set up a table for the service provider to place business cards and literature at the entrance to the rehearsal dinner, reception, or wedding for guests to look at in exchange for a discount. If the person is interested, but does not know what type of discount to offer, suggest a pre-planned discount based on your budget. For example if the photographers would normally charge you $2,300 for their service, state that you can only afford $2,000 (a little more than a 10% discount). However, inform them that you are willing to allow the photographer to market his services in exchange for the difference. The service providers may try to counter offer the amount of the discount, but only accept the offer if you are comfortable with the discount.

Although you may think guests will think you are cheap by allowing service providers to market themselves at your wedding, it can be done in a very inconspicuous way. For example, if you have a guest book available at the entrance to your reception, arrange the table in the following manner. First, have a large table available so that the guest book and the marketing materials are not converging on each other. Be sure to have sufficient space between the two, but not so much as to offend the marketers. Then have small signs placed on the table that introduce the marketer. For example, you may have a sign that states "Photography Service Provided by John and Terry's PhotoWorld". Then in front of the sign have a business card holder and/or brochures from the company.

Other services can also be marketed in different locations. For example, prior to the cake cutting, the cake provider can place a similar marketing scheme as discussed in the previous paragraph on the cake table. Then when the cake cutting is ready to start, remove the marketing material to ensure that it will not show up in your photographs.